You Have To Get Your Own Saint

You Have To Get Your Own Saint

✦

A Memoir of Two Years in Spain

Kristen Hestir

iUniverse, Inc.
New York Lincoln Shanghai

You Have To Get Your Own Saint
A Memoir of Two Years in Spain

iUniverse books may be ordered through booksellers or by contacting:

iUniverse
2021 Pine Lake Road, Suite 100
Lincoln, NE 68512
www.iuniverse.com
1-800-Authors (1-800-288-4677)

ISBN-13: 978-0-595-39259-9 (pbk)
ISBN-13: 978-0-595-83654-3 (ebk)
ISBN-10: 0-595-39259-8 (pbk)
ISBN-10: 0-595-83654-2 (ebk)

Printed in the United States of America

This book is dedicated to Brigitte.
Thank you for your friendship.

Contents

Introduction

Two years ago, my husband and I lost our jobs. We had been living and working in Norway for many years. Although only in our mid-forties, we dreamed of an early retirement. In order to turn the dream into reality we needed a warmer, cheaper place to live. Having spent a few vacations in Barcelona, we set our hearts on Spain. We searched for books on what it was really like for an ordinary middleclass foreigner to live in there. We found books for tourists, books on how to buy a property, how to restore an old farmhouse and finding a holiday home but nothing about making a permanent move. Thousands of foreigners move to Spain every year. What was the feel and texture of day in, day out living for these people? Our search for information was in vain but we blindly made the move anyway.

This book is a diary of our first two years in Spain. The people are real and the events true but they are from my memory, someone else might remember them differently. I have changed the names of the people to protect their privacy. The first years in a new country are always transitional years fraught with excitement, frustration, delight, culture shock and exasperation! This book demanded to be written. I had little choice in the matter. If you are planning a new life in Spain, I hope this book is helpful. I wish you luck and happiness on your adventure.

Welcome to Spain

I'm a nervous wreck waiting for the cats to come off the luggage belt at the *Barcelona* airport. After a year of dreaming and planning we've sold almost everything we own, said farewell to jobs and friends and now we are here, finally, here in Spain. Soon we see the cats and Dennis leaps over the first conveyor belt, grabs their cages and passes them to me. Both cats are hollering, "MEOW! MEOW!" We can hear their loud cries even over the noisy passengers waiting for luggage. Everyone stares at us, some people are smiling and some come over, kneel down and wiggle their fingers through the wires of the cages. They ask us if the cats are OK and we nod our heads yes. Our cats don't appreciate their good intentions. Afraid of strangers, they squeeze themselves into tiny balls and huddle as far back in the cage as possible. We stop at customs to show their rabies certificates but the agent isn't interested. He barely glances at the documents then waves us through.

We pick up our rental car and head out of town. We have only a tourist map to guide us north of Barcelona to the town of *LLoret de Mar* where we have rented a house. I forgot to pack our maps. Everything we need to live on during the next few months, including cat food, litter box, bedding and towels are in our two suitcases. We exit the airport following the signs toward *Girona*[1] and five minutes down the road we're stuck in a traffic jam. Two lanes are trying to exit, two lanes are trying to merge and everyone else wants to be where they are not. It's chaos. Dennis stops to let a truck merge. He has no choice since the truck is going to merge whether we like it or not. The guy in the truck behind us gets pissed off, drives on the shoulder to our right. He's yelling at us and shaking his fist out the window. Then he cuts in front of us. I'm white knuckling the door handle but Dennis just laughs. "I don't think he's saying, 'Welcome to Spain.'"

I remember a conversation I had with a man who lived in Barcelona. He recommended that we forget having a car in Spain. "Use a motorcycle instead" he said. "The climate is good and there's absolutely no parking in the city. I used to own a car but one day I got stuck in traffic for five hours and decided then and

---

1.   Northern Catalunya's largest city, spelled Gerona in Castilian Spanish.

there to sell the car and buy a motorcycle." I'm hoping this is not one of those five-hour traffic jams.

About thirty minutes later we start moving again, slowly making our way through the heavy traffic of Barcelona. The cats are quiet in the back seat proba-bly relieved by the quiet of the car and the air conditioning. It's more than an hour before we exit the city and hit the A7 expressway heading north. Luckily, we changed money at the airport. This is an expensive toll road. The traffic is light and moves fast. We drive the speed limit of 120 kph. It seems to be the minimum so we stay in the slow lane. Cars fly past.

My husband, Dennis, was here a month ago looking for a house to rent. He took photos of the highway signs that will lead us to our rented house. We chose this part of *Catalunya*[2] because of the climate, the green hilly country and the proximity to Barcelona. He's studied the photos and recognizes the highway exits so we reach the *urbanización* or subdivision, where we will be living with little trouble.

We drive up a hill, twisting and turning through narrow concrete streets lined with brick houses. All the properties here are gated and guarded by growling dogs. When we arrive at the house, two dogs run toward us snapping and barking through the gate. Dennis tries the gate handle and it's locked. We stare at each other, not sure what we should do. I realize that I have the phone number for Marta, our landlady, in an email but forgot to write it down or put it in our mobile phones. As if on cue, a red car pulls up behind us and Marta gets out. She has brown hair, is pale, of medium build and is quite attractive. She's from the Netherlands but following the Spanish form of greeting, she gives us a kiss on each cheek. We are a little surprised by this warm, greeting. After living in Nor-way for eleven years, we are accustomed to the standoffish, stiff handshakes of the Scandinavians. Marta explains that she has hired someone to clean the house but they of course are late, and since we are early, the house is a mess. She ties up the barking dogs and walks us through the house. We put our cats in the back bed-room and let them out of their cages, give them food, water and most important their litter box. Marta is right; the house is a mess. There are clothes, papers, trash and dirty dishes lying around plus there's a big hole in the kitchen wall. Marta explains that a man is coming soon to install a new water heater in the house; i.e. there is no hot water. I silently hope this isn't one of those horror stories I've heard about Spain where six months from now we are taking cold showers and

---

2.   Catalunya is a small triangle of northeastern Spain, bordering France and the Medi-terranean Sea. It is spelled Cataluña in Castillian Spanish and Catalonia in English

still waiting for the plumber. Within the hour, both the cleaning lady and the plumber arrive. We sit on the porch on plastic lawn furniture and wait for them to finish. Marta leaves to pick up her kids at school but promises to return later. It's sunny and warm and there's a beautiful view from the house, though a little hazy. The house sits high on a mountain ridge with a view to the southwest of a huge mountain peak, *Mt. Montseny*. At 1700 meters, it dominates the horizon. Today the mountain peak is dark and covered with clouds. The surrounding country has lush, green rolling hills.

I decide to take a walk through this *urbanización* where we have rented a house for a year. The empty lots around the house are crammed with flowers, pines, cork oaks, birds and insects. The cork trees look strange, like they've been given bowl haircuts; every one has been stripped of bark from shoulder height down. The streets ramble up and down the hillsides. The country to the east seems unspoiled, a vast canopy of gray-green cork oak. I can barely make out the Mediterranean through the haze. The houses are a mix of immaculate and ruin; a mansion sitting next to a hovel. Lovely brick homes with tile terraces and swimming pools stand next to shacks of corrugated tin with plastic taped across the windows. People are out walking the streets and everyone I pass greets me with *buenas* or the Catalan equivalent *bon dia*. At the bottom of the hill there's a restaurant and a small grocery store called a *super mercat*. I pull on the door but the market is closed, it's lunch hour. There is a swimming pool behind the restaurant but it's October and this late in the year it's closed. There are recycling bins in the parking lot in front of the restaurant but people have been careless. There are plastic bags lying all over the ground ravaged by dogs. There's trash scattered everywhere. I'm certainly not in pristine Norway any longer.

Marta returns late in the afternoon with her boyfriend Carlos and her kids, Jon and Elise. Carlos is Spanish and they met about a year ago. He's stout with brown hair, brown eyes and creamy brown skin. He has a disarming smile and speaks English hesitantly. Jon is nine years old and Elise is seven. They both have Marta's curly brown hair. They speak Dutch, Catalan and Spanish and a little French but no English. Marta looks up and down the road for our non-existent moving van, offering to help us unload our truck. Unfortunately, we explain, we don't have a truck to unload. We told them that we would be bringing our household goods down from Norway but we could not find a truck to rent. Marta and Carlos are shocked since they have moved out the washing machine, refrigerator and microwave. I explain that I couldn't find a moving company in Norway either. I tried six or seven companies who advertised international moving. The closest I got was a man who asked me, "*Har du tenkt å flytte dette år?*"

Were you thinking of moving this year? So, our goods are in storage in Norway and everything we will live on for the next months is in two suitcases and two backpacks.

The cleaning lady is finished and we walk through the house. The front of the house has a covered and tiled porch with orange flowered rattan furniture. The front porch opens into the living room with a small sofa and a stone lined fireplace in the corner. There is a tiny kitchen behind the living room, just room for one person to stand and cook. The kitchen has no oven only a butane gas stove. To the left of the living room there is a small dining room with Ikea wooden table and chairs. There are two bedrooms on the west side, obviously late additions because you have to walk through the bathroom to reach them. Marta leaves us the sofa, dining table and bed. I like Marta and Carlos instantly. They both have a manner that puts us at ease. They are generous and loan us bed covers, pillows and some towels until we can get settled.

In the late afternoon, we drive to the *super mercat* at the bottom of the *urbanización* and stock up on cat food, bottled water, dried pasta and canned tomatoes. With no refrigerator we avoid anything that is perishable. We will buy a refrigerator and washing machine and take them with us when we buy our own home. The next day, on Marta's recommendation, we head down to the nearby town of *Blanes* to look for a place to fill the butane tank and to buy a refrigerator. We forget that, in Spain, everything closes for a few hours in the afternoon. We arrive just as the shops are closing. Within minutes the town is dead, not a soul on the street. We decide to stay and eat *menu del dia,* the set menu, at the seaside in *Blanes.* We both order seafood and though reasonable in price it's unremarkable in quality. As we finish our meal it's nearly 3:00 in the afternoon and we are the only ones in the restaurant. We wander around the quiet town until the shops begin to open and check on the prices of appliances. We look at two small appliance stores finally choosing a simple Spanish brand refrigerator. We get some extra keys made for our house and gate at the *ferrertería* and head back home. On the way out of *Blanes* we spot a *butano* supply, hundreds of orange butane bottles stacked on pallets on the side of the road. Most of the houses in Spain use butane for cooking and for hot water. Some also use it for heating. When I lived for a month in the heart of Barcelona's old town I was awakened every morning by men yelling down the narrow streets *BUTAN...O! BUTAN...O!* Like the Spanish version of a yodel, it took me the whole month to figure out what they were saying. We stop to exchange our empty bottles for full ones and I see 'Warning Flammable!' signs everywhere. I'm shocked to see the attendant smoking a cigarette as he loads our gas bottle in the car. I know I will get used to this, but now

I'm paranoid as hell driving with a full bottle of gas in the trunk of the car and am relieved to get home.

Marta and Carlos visit the next day. Carlos wants to show me around the garden. I love gardening and look forward to the long growing season here in *Catalunya*. The house has a large terraced garden. The lower level has been left wild. There's a swing set for the kids and a couple of dilapidated doghouses. The second level has an old chicken coop; some fruit trees, thick gnarled grape vines and a large vegetable garden overgrown with grass and weeds. There are tomato plants and sweet peppers staked with tepees of old bamboo. There are onions, chard, celery and some dying squash plants. Carlos has good English and as he enthusiastically shows me each plant, he keeps apologizing for the state of the garden. He explains that he never gardened before last year. "The garden has very good soil. The old owner bring it here with big trucks. The neighbors kept telling me to garden so I decide to try. I don't know if it's correct."

I think the garden looks pretty good. The tomatoes, chard and peppers are still producing. As far as I'm concerned, if you can eat from your garden it has been a success. Neat and tidy is icing on the cake. Carlos shows me how to prune the grape vine, also knowledge gleaned from the neighbors. As he clips the twisted branches, he tells me he is leaving in a few weeks to work in Andorra for the winter. "I don't really want to work all winter but right now I and Marta fight a lot. I hope maybe Marta miss me if I go," he tells me. After the tour Marta and Carlos invite us to visit them for lunch on Sunday. Carlos will cook us *paella* but he explains, "My *paella* is not good like my mother's." As Carlos is leaving he becomes shy about his *paella*. "Maybe not we have *paella*. Maybe I make hamburgers instead."

I'm disappointed and tell him, "Don't be shy now, we want to try it."

The next day we drive to *Girona* to register for an NIE number for Dennis. This is in essence a Spanish social security number for foreigners. *Girona* is a very pleasant city with a large park and a river separating the old town from the new. From the narrow cobblestone streets of the old town it seems prosperous with designer shops interspersed with pricey restaurants. We stop at the tourist information office to find out where to register. They give us a map and send us to the municipal police station where we have to go through a security check and stand in a long, slow queue. We finally talk to someone in our halting Spanish. They can't understand a word we say, but as soon as they see Dennis's Norwegian passport they tell us that we are in the wrong office. They grab our map and point out the right location. Dennis has another long wait while I go to a nearby café and have a *café solo,* a strong, dark coffee with two heaping spoonfuls of sugar. Dennis comes out very satisfied. Everything went smoothly considering he speaks so little Spanish and they speak so little English. Many people hire a *gestor*, a solicitor specializing in Spanish law, when they need to deal with the government. Not only do *gestors* understand the paperwork, they have those all-important personal connections. To save money we have decided to try first on our own and only resort to a *gestor* if we can't manage. Dennis is told he will have to wait two weeks for his NIE number. This number is needed before we can register our residence at the city hall, open a bank account, get a telephone, health insurance and buy a car.

On Sunday, we drive to the little town of *Vidreres* for lunch with Marta and Carlos. After greeting us with kisses, they hand us glasses of red wine. Dennis refuses, "I'm driving." he explains.

Carlos is surprised. "We Spanish would never say that! We drink and drive. It's what we do. We don't even think about it."

We used to be the same when we lived in America but Norway has such strict alcohol laws that now we simply don't do it. They have a town house on a narrow street in the village. The house is long and narrow and two levels. They share walls with the neighbors on two sides so there are only windows on the front and back of the house. It has been completely renovated and is light and airy. The house looks so new, I'm surprise to see part of the tile in the hallway is torn up. Marta tells me that she almost didn't buy the house. There was a water leak on the day of the closing and I almost walked away from the whole thing until the old owners promised to get it fixed. "Now look still not fixed!"

Lunch with Marta and Carlos is delicious. We have *paella*, wine and a Catalan favorite; *pa amb tomáquet*; a piece of bread grilled on an open flame then rubbed with fresh garlic cloves, fresh tomato and drizzled with olive oil. We sit at a picnic table in their back yard under an umbrella. The yard is small and hot, with weeds growing among discarded construction materials. Marta explains that they want to put in a tile patio then some plants maybe some trees for shade but first the laundry room has to be finished. She points to an unfinished brick wall jutting out from the kitchen. It's about three feet high with a roof on it. "That will be the laundry room."

"Outdoors?" I ask.

"Oh yes, that's how they do it here."

It's relaxing and easy to be with them. Marta is frustrated with the flies we are constantly shooing from our faces and from the food on the table. She tells me it's because the old woman who lives next door raises chickens. "I get to buy fresh eggs from her, but look at all these flies! I guess I have to take the good with the bad."

Carlos gets lively after a few glasses of wine. He has to go into work in a few hours. He works at the front desk of a four star hotel in *Lloret de Mar*. He tells us that the last time he went to work drunk he had fun teasing three little old ladies from Valencia about watching porno films on TV. "They give you one minute of porno free, but after that you have to pay. So I tell these old ladies: 'You were watching those porno films.' They shake their heads and deny it. My colleagues are laughing behind me when I tell the ladies, 'I can see on the computer that you were watching those films!' They shake their heads very strong, 'No, no, no, no, no, we didn't.'" Laughing he tells us, "I loved teasing those little ladies…their faces, they become a red color."

The next day we drive to *Lloret* and return our rental car. We'll be using a bus until we can buy a car, but we can't buy a car without an NIE number and a bank account. Luckily, a small city bus runs eight times a day between *Lloret* and our neighborhood.

Two weeks later Dennis's NIE number is ready. The first major hurdle is over. Next, he will apply for *residencia,* a residence permit, which will give him permission to live and work here for five years. We also have to register ourselves as residents at the town hall, or *ayuntamiento,* of *Lloret*. The clerk speaks no English and we have problems understanding. I think he's asking, "Have you registered before?" but Dennis understands him to be asking, "Do you want to register?" Each time I answer, "*No*" while Dennis simultaneously answers, "*Sí*". The clerk asks us the question four more times and each time I answer, "*No*" and Dennis answers, "*Sí.*" I can't figure out why Dennis keeps saying yes. The man gives up and looks at our paperwork and tells us to go make some copies. On the way to make copies we try to figure out what was wrong. Dennis says even if the guy repeated 40 million times he still wouldn't understand the question. I don't go in with him when we deliver our copies. Everything goes smoothly, he walks away registered.

Prostitutes, Spanish Classes and Buying a Burro

We're living in an unfinished *urbanización*. One thing we discover is that here, on the Spanish coasts the construction is endless, whether it is commercial buildings, roads or private housing. There are empty lots for sale everywhere and properties in all stages of development. So much of the work seems to be done by the owners themselves. What an odd sequence they build in. In America and Scandinavia, the house is built first and then the garage. If there is money left over, the landscaping and fencing is finished. It's just the opposite here. The fencing and gate are built first then the land is terraced and lined with potted trees and plants. The garage is built next and becomes a temporary home while the foundation is poured for the house and finally the house comes last. It's not unusual to see an extended family on Sunday afternoons sitting in lawn chairs grilling meat next to an unfinished garage surrounded by racks of drying laundry using an ice chest for a refrigerator. The obligatory family dog is jumping and barking and the family is laughing and pointing and discussing the soon to be built *casa unifamilia*.

Driving between *Girona* and *Barcelona* on the slower national highway we pass through farmland, industrial areas and wilderness slashed by ravines. There's the occasional young woman standing provocatively on the roadside. I'm trying to convince myself that with their short skirts and catwalk poses they are just trying to get a ride but I know they are prostitutes. Every time Dennis sees one he says, "there's another girl waiting for the bus." This is what he will tell his mother when she visits. I try to imagine what has driven a girl to such desperation. I remember reading an article in *Aftenposten*, an Oslo newspaper, about a seventeen-year-old middle class, ordinary girl who hitchhiked around her neighborhood selling sex. She did it to earn money to buy the right kind of clothes. She told her parents that the clothes were borrowed from friends when they saw her wearing something new. She said that the first few times she had sex with a stranger, it made her want to vomit but the money was very good. She learned to close everything out of her mind but the vision of that new jacket. We pass another girl with curly dark hair, tight jeans and a bare midriff combing her hair and putting on eye makeup on the side of the road. From a distance, she's stunningly beautiful. I can't believe these girls are doing this just to buy some new clothes. I realize that I can't make up a story about her or any of these women. I've never been desperate enough to begin to understand.

I ask Carlos if it's more proper to say *buenas dias* or *hola* when you pass someone on the street. He says he likes to break the ice with *hola* even with old people. He especially likes to do it with tourists who know only three expressions, *buenas dias, buenas noches* and *adios*, "I just say *hola* to disturb them a little and make them relax. It's what we Spanish like to do."

The Spanish love to talk and can stretch even the simplest conversation into an elaborate discussion. Waiting in line takes forever as each person has a lengthy discourse with the person behind the counter. Even a simple yes or no turns into, "*Si, si, si, si, si, si, si, si*" or "*No, no, no, no, no, no.*" We read about this chattiness before we arrived and I'm determined to relax and not let it bother me. I try to use the time to listen to the conversations, small lessons in Spanish or Catalan.

One day while looking for a birthday present for my mother I have to wait in a shop for twenty minutes just to ask if they have a different size. Dennis is waiting in the street outside tapping his foot. Soon he will start pacing. The clerk is chatting with a woman so intensely that I don't dare interrupt. With nothing to do but eavesdrop, I hear the words for potatoes and onions. It dawns on me that they are discussing recipes while I wait.

They use the word *vale* for everything so I look this up in the dictionary. The verb means **to be worth** or **to cost** but it obviously has other uses like: OK…thanks…can I help you? Next…I agree…I understand…. do you understand?…here you are…see you later. Within a few weeks I'm using this word too, my first habit in Spanish.

We must learn to adjust to this strange daily schedule. We've taken the bus twice into *Lloret de Mar* to find it completely closed down, a literal ghost town. From 1:00 to 4:00 there's not a thing open except restaurants, even the buses stop running for an afternoon break. The Spanish take lunch very seriously and use it to eat well, visit with their families and take a nap. I asked Marta if she had a hard time getting used to it. She said not at all. It fits her just fine, especially that little nap in the afternoon. "Carl Jung, you know the famous psychologist? He used to sit at his desk in the afternoon after a morning of hard work, hold a spoon over his head with one hand and close his eyes then slowly doze off. When he relaxed so much that the spoon dropped on his head and woke him up, he started work again totally refreshed. I'm a spoon person too. A short nap like that gives me so much energy for the rest of the day."

I'm sitting outside the house at 9:00 on a Friday morning. It's late November and the sun is warming up my black sweatshirt so I'm almost hot. Soon I will have to change to something lighter. We've had two weeks of cool rainy weather-much cooler than I expected. We had winds of 100 km an hour yesterday and now I can see the damage it has done. The rose bushes are stripped bare and branches are broken from trees, a potted begonia was blown off the veranda and lies broken on the ground, the four-o'clocks are lying on their sides. Nonetheless, it's a beautiful morning now and I listen for the sounds around me, trying to decide if they are particularly Spanish. There's some background traffic noise, a motorcycle whining up the road, the sound of a radio muffled in the distance, two birds squabbling in a tree; sounds from any city, anywhere. Then I hear a chain saw, the tap, tap, tapping of a bricklayer up the road, a construction worker breaking out in song at the top of his lungs, a turkey gobble. These I think are particularly Spanish. There seems to be incessant building everywhere, and chain saws are used to strip the land of vegetation before the build. The mountain we live on is scarred with roads, as are all the mountains around. There are lots are in all degrees of preparation for building with signs everywhere "*en vende*", for sale. There seems to be little regard for erosion. Everywhere that we walk we see retaining walls in need of repair, yards washed out, and roads slumping, as the land beneath them crumbles away. A few days ago, Dennis walked down the road to put our trash in the bin and the bins were gone. He could see them lying in the ravine far below. The curb where they had stood was missing, only it's rebar remained hanging in the air, the road next to it completely gone. We remind ourselves not to buy anything in this *urbanización* although we think it's beautiful and we are comfortable here. I finally pull myself away from the sunshine and get up to sweep the remains of the shattered clay pot.

Suddenly I remember that yesterday was Thanksgiving. I missed it completely! With no decorations or advertising to remind me, no way for our families to call, I simply forgot. Some American holidays like Halloween and Valentine's Day have migrated to Europe, but Thanksgiving is strictly American. In Norway, I had an American friend who always had a big Thanksgiving dinner with at least twenty guests. In the true spirit of the holiday, she would ask everyone to bring something; food or wine or chairs or whatever they could manage. Every year she would have her daughter tell the story of Thanksgiving; about how the Indians saved the lives of the pilgrims by sharing their food. Then she would thank the guests for their contributions. The Norwegians loved seeing a side of America that was about sharing rather than shopping.

Lloret de Mar is a strange town. On the inland side they are building, block after block of high-rise apartments. Construction cranes fill the air. Near the city center the town is bisected by a busy main street which ends right at the Mediterranean Sea. There's a pedestrian zone of narrow streets filled with clothing and shoe shops, banks, moneychangers, bars and bakeries. The main street, which is opened to traffic, is lined with high-rise hotels, tacky tourist shops and restaurants advertising in German, French, English and Dutch. There are arcades and discos, casinos, ice cream parlors, miniature golf, travel centers, liquor stores and even a Burger King. The town is tawdry and tacky. We've read that the city once promoted itself as a party town but soon discovered that rowdy brawls and drunken vandalism comes with that type of tourist. The city has tried to remake its image and attract a different clientele but reputations are difficult to change.

Tour buses cruise the streets day and night. Standing on the main street we can see buses from Germany, England, France, even Sweden. We find two redeeming features in *Lloret*. A small section on the main street, on top of the city-parking garage is lined with old palm trees and has a large old fashioned carousel. It's ornately gilded with white and black and pink ceramic stallions. It sits quietly to one side of the square only open for a few hours on weekends, I'm happy to see it still appeals to children of all ages. One Friday evening we watch them running up and down the aisles trying to find the best horse to climb before the music begins. *Lloret's* other redeeming feature is the beach. It's a classic half moon shape, studded at each end with small rocky cliffs, covered in palms, cork oak and flowers. The sand is perfect. There are public showers and beach chairs, umbrellas and ice cream stands. Walking the beach and nearby cliffs you can sense the sleepy fishing village this town once was, but it's a fleeting sensation drowned out by the sound of a honking taxi or street vendor hawking his wares.

We meet Carol, a British woman who runs an English bookshop in *Lloret de Mar* with her husband. She is the quintessential chatterbox who we find delightful and helpful. They, like us, have disregarded the advice to try living here about a year before you pull up your roots at home. They explain, "We have two children. You can't pull your kids out of school force them to learn Catalan for a year and then change your mind. You've got to just decide it's going to work and do it." Our excuse is simpler; we don't have the money to keep a home in Norway and Spain. We are determined to make this our home.

Carol gives us a tip on a cheap adult Spanish course so we go to the *Escole d'Adults* in *Lloret* to sign up. The doors are open and a few classes are in session, but we can't find anyone in the office to talk to. Back at home I call the school but get an answering machine in Spanish or Catalan which I can't understand. I ring Marta and ask her to call for us. A few days later Marta phones to tell us that we need to go sign up for classes now. They are completely full but she has talked the professor into letting Dennis and I into the January course. She tells us to press them if they refuse. The secretary at the school scowls like a troll when we tell her we want to sign up for classes. She speaks no English but she taps a list with her hand and tells us it's impossible, the classes are full. A woman comes out from the back room and asks if a lady rang for us yesterday. She speaks slow, clear Spanish and she lets us sign up for the class. There are already 30 or 40 names on the list and we are grateful to get in.

We have to take the local bus into town to do our shopping. The bus goes to *Lloret* where it's expensive to shop compared to the smaller towns inland. We have no choice until we buy a car. The bus seats about fifteen people and is nearly always full. The bus crowd is lively and chatty and we are the only ones who don't join in. Tonight, as I ride home from my shopping trip, the bus driver teases some children sitting in the front of the bus. The children are squealing with delight. When they get off, the driver gets out of the bus and continues the game. There are peals of laughter coming from the street. I think how unusual it is to have a bus driver play with children during work. I wonder if this would ever happen in a small town in Norway or in America.

We finally get a telephone connected at Marta's house. It feels like we are back in the world after a long retreat, six weeks completely incommunicado; no telephone, no Internet, no car, no TV, no radio, no friends. We want to get an internet connection immediately. It's my connection to family and friends in America and Norway. They are pushing broadband here but it seems very expensive, the same as Norwegian prices. We opt for old-fashioned 56k modem connection and hope it will be good enough. At the *Telefonica* store the woman refuses to give us this old connection. She says something in Spanish but I only catch two words; *burro* and *coche*. Then I realize she's telling us: why buy a burro when you could have a car? We decide to try to sign up directly with *Telefonica* from an Internet café. We spend the next hour reading *Telefonica* web pages trying to figure out which service to sign up for and finally pick one that sounds right. We don't know the acronyms *RDSI*, *RTB* and *RTC*. We try to sign up and get a message that the service is not offered for our telephone number. We go through the same routine with another Internet provider, Tiscali. This time we are denied because we do not have a *DNI* number. A *DNI,* is a social security number for nationals, Dennis has only an *NIE,* a social security number for foreigners. We decide to try another *Telefonica* shop and see if we have better luck. In two minutes, we walk out with a free internet connection CD. No wonder the previous shop did not want to give us a disc, it was free. Within a half hour of arriving home we are online. So simple, yet so difficult.

Why Are We Here?

Almost a year ago I lost my job in Norway. I was one of the thousands hit by the cutbacks in the telecom industry. The last few years at work had been chaotic with departments closing left and right and rumors of layoffs rampant. I should have looked for another job before the big crash came, but even that wasn't safe. There were stories about people starting new jobs then losing them within a few months. I was comfortable, perhaps too comfortable, in my job. I'd been at the same company for eighteen years and thought longevity would give me a little protection. It didn't. Three years earlier I'd cut my work hours to 60%, three days a week. I still worked a lot of overtime when needed but that extra free time was extremely precious to me. I finally had time to write and to garden. I didn't want to loose it. When my department was finally closed, I knew I would never find another part time job. It would be difficult to find a job at all, with hundreds of engineers competing for every available position; I would never be able to ask for part time. A few days after I was laid off, Dennis, who also worked in the telecom industry, lost his job too.

We loved our lives, our house, our jobs and living in Norway. Dennis, born in America, had even applied for Norwegian citizenship. We'd first come to Norway on short-term contracts but that had long since expired. We had our permanent residency. This was our home. Our lives were suddenly turned upside down. The thought of working full time turned my stomach. The free time was much more important to me than the money. But did I, did we, have a choice?

Like thousand of Scandinavians we had dreamed of someday escaping the long winters and retiring to sunny Spain but we were only in our forties, a long way from retirement. If we cashed in all our chips, sold everything and lived frugally could we retire early and live off our savings? We'd been able to pay off our mortgage five years earlier and had invested all our extra money in ultra safe Norwegian government bonds. If we are extremely careful with the money that we earn on selling the house maybe we can buy a home in Spain and live off the remainder plus our interest income.

What a dilemma! Scramble to find new work, work forty or more hours a week and keep our lifestyle OR risk everything, sell our house, leave Norway, move to a country we know little about and retire.

We began to scan the Internet for real estate in Spain and watched the housing prices. We searched for books on living in Spain. We tried to find out what life was like especially for foreigners. Could we really afford to retire at the age of 46? It began to seem feasible. We looked for jobs in Norway but our hearts weren't in it. A paradigm shift had taken place in our hearts and minds. I decided to become certified to teach English and traveled to Barcelona for the month long training classes. I could teach English part time in Spain to stretch our money. I took a trip and explored southern Spain; *Malaga, Seville, Granada* and *Córdova.* I rejected them all; after living in Norway they were a shock to my system, too hot and too dry. Dennis went to *Catalunya* and looked at house prices in *Girona* then down the coast toward *Tarragona.* He had to cut his trip short—robbed of everything at the train station in *Tarragona.* Now we had second thoughts. Do we really want to leave, nice safe Norway for a country where we have to worry about being robbed? I studied Spanish. Dennis received his Norwegian citizenship, ironically making a move to Spain possible. Americans can't simply move to any country in Europe. We need an employer to sponsor us, to be independently wealthy, or pensioners with retirement income. Norwegians however, like other Europeans, can move freely within Europe. One day we realized that our minds were made up, we were going.

It took a year but we finally sold our home and most of our furniture. We sold our car and said goodbye to our friends in Norway. Now, here we are in *Catalunya.*

As soon as Dennis receives his residency, we will try to buy a house. Our budget only allows for one year of renting. I scan the real estate catalogues and the Internet for houses. All our planning now seems pointless; the prices have increased enormously in the last year. There is so much for sale but 99% of it is out of our price range. Shockingly the prices here rival the most expensive suburbs of Oslo with many houses selling for more than 300,000 Euro. It hurts to pay that in Norway where building techniques are very good. It seems crazy to pay that here where building techniques can range from incompetent, to dubious, to downright foolish. How do you know, once the façade is on, which one you've purchased?

There are *en vende*, for sale, signs everywhere. We look at prices in this area just to get an idea of the market. We know we will try to go inland where the prices suit our budget. We see signs for *estiercol en vende*. What are they? Apartments or studios for sale? We find out later that *estiercol* means manure. We're glad we did not call and ask for a showing. We stop in at a few agents and ask about some of the cheaper houses (selling for under 120,000 Euro) posted in their windows. They won't give out the address even in our own *urbanización* unless we make an appointment for them to show us around. There is no multiple listing, no common database for houses for sale. It's a very competitive market. Many agents will not even post signs on the houses they have for sale because other agents will try to entice away the sellers. We read a story about a British couple that bought a house for 200,000 Euro with a promise from a Spanish bank to loan them 90% of the mortgage. After signing a contract, the bank evaluated the property at 140,000 Euro and would only loan 90% of that. Now the couple is stuck with a house they can't afford. OK, they made a bad contract. They should have inserted a clause "on condition of financing." What scares me more than signing a bad contract is the fact that someone could buy a house for 60,000 Euro more than it's worth and not realize it.

Finding a Friend

The smallest task is difficult when you can't speak a language. We panic if the phone rings and argue with each other about whose turn it is to answer. Being less willing to miss a call, I usually lose this battle. Making a simple doctor's appointment or opening a bank account creates enormous stress. I don't know what I would do without Marta. She helps us order wood for the fireplace, get signed up for Spanish class; she calls the electric company when our power goes out (which is often in the winter months). She shows us the best and cheapest places to shop, where to eat breakfast, the cheapest *patisserie* in *Lloret* for coffee and pastries. She explains how to apply for health care and a library card where we can check out free videos. She tells us about the weekly markets in *Lloret* and *Vidreres*, the best places to buy fruit, vegetables and plants. She pours through real estate catalogues for us and calls agents to make appointments to look at houses. While Dennis is out of town, she joins me in viewing houses and helps me communicate with the agents in Spanish. How did we get so lucky to find this person?

Marta often comes over in the morning for coffee and croissants and we talk about living here, writing, teaching, learning Spanish. Like us, she loves to read and we talk often about the latest books we are reading. She has an extensive library of books in five languages, ranging from classics to the latest best sellers and loans them out with enthusiasm. She is a writer too, also unpublished, and we talk about the stories we are writing, about the writing craft.

She is very busy with her children and teaching and is disorganized, inevitably forgetting something when she visits. She's always misplacing her mobile telephone or losing her keys. She is one of the most open people I have ever met, completely unaffected. She has such a positive attitude that it is infectious. Even when complaining about the Netherlands government or the Catholic Church she does it with humor. She explains to me that she can have quite a temper and it suddenly comes out of nowhere, but she chuckles at herself as she explains. I feel like I have known her for years. She's become a friend.

Want to Drive?

It's been difficult to shop for cars without having a car. The buses stop in the center of town and the car dealers tend to be on the outskirts. We rent a car for one day just to make the task easier. We want to buy from a dealer so they will handle all the paper work and in the hope we can get insurance through them too. Although it's cheaper here than Norway, there's a tax on used cars that keeps the prices fairly high.

Finally, Dennis looks at a car at the Peugeot dealer in *Girona* and wants me to test drive it. We take the bus to *Girona* and the bus driver is kind enough to make an unscheduled stop at the auto dealer and let us off. We stand looking at the car for a few minutes when the salesman arrives and starts reciting his sales pitch, a stream of Spanish (or Catalan?) pours from his mouth as he's waving and pointing at the car. A few minutes into the recital he suddenly stops and asks, "*Me entiendeis?*" Do you understand me? We laugh and shake our heads no. He pauses for a minute, not sure of what to do, then motions as if he's grabbing a steering wheel and asks in English, "Want to drive?" I get into the driver's seat then reach into my purse to try to show him my driver's license. He doesn't want to see it, "I'm not police," he tells me.

We agree to buy the car and insurance and go to the bank to make the payment. We are asked to come back after lunch when all the paperwork will be ready. Not even a business deal should interfere with a good Spanish lunch. We walk the few kilometers into the center of *Girona* and eat at a nice café by the river. The food and service are very good and we are still surprised by how cheap the food is. For six euro each we have wine, a small dish of lasagna for an appetizer, *bacalao* (salted cod), with roasted vegetables for a main course and chocolate pudding and coffee for desert. After eating lunch we walk to the old city and the cathedral. The doors to the cathedral are open and we go inside for a look. It's a mixture of architectural styles Baroque, Gothic, Romanesque with beautiful round petal shaped stained glass windows letting in the only light. Outside the church we climb stairs to the top of the old wall surrounding the old city. From here we have a nice *vista* of the city. It's much larger than it feels. We both really like *Girona*. It's difficult to identify just what makes it so appealing but we both agree-it has something. We wander the small cobblestone streets. All of the shops are closed for lunch but I can tell most of them are exclusive and pricey. As the clock nears 4:00, we walk to the train station to find a taxicab back to the car dealer. About an hour later we are driving home in a new used car.

It took one day to get our first dent. We decided to see some of *Catalunya* and drove down to the coastal town of *Blanes*, inland to *Tordera* and then up into the hills to the small town of *Breda*, famous for pottery.

Blanes is directly south of *Lloret*. It has the only hospital for miles around and unlike *Lloret* has industry apart from tourism. It once had one of the largest textile factories in Spain, offering jobs to people from *Andalucía* and *Extramadora,* the poorer regions of Spain. Unlike other cities in *Catalunya*, a large part of the population speaks *Castellano*, not the regional language Catalan. Many of the factories have closed down but the town is still thriving. In the winter months *Lloret* becomes a ghost town, most of the shops and restaurants close, but in *Blanes* the shops are open and full of people.

Tordera, a small industrial town just inland from *Blanes*, is a little cheaper and less touristy than the coastal towns. Carlos has told me that if we want to find the center of town, always look for the church and *Tordera* is no exception. The old city center has cobblestone streets winding around a small hill crowned by an old stone church. There are massive construction projects underway with new subdivisions and apartment blocks being built on the outskirts. We like the old part of town but today the valley is filled with heavy brown air and there are vile smells in the air.

The drive to *Breda* is quite beautiful with the Peak of *Montseny* Mountain in the background. What a contrast it is to the unspoiled beauty of Norway. Almost anywhere you live, even near Oslo, you are only a few kilometers from a pristine forest. In the winter we used to have moose sleep in our front yard. Moose! Here it feels like the land has been cultivated forever, there's not a speck of untouched earth. Even the "forests" have been planted; the trees are lined up in tidy perpendicular rows all the same size. Nonetheless, the autumn colors are fantastic with bright yellow and orange leaves filling the valleys and the gray green cork oak on the hilltops above.

Breda is a quaint little town with pottery shops lining the main thoroughfare. We find a place to park in a neighborhood a few streets off the main highway and wander around for about an hour looking in shop windows and getting a feel for the place. It seems more reserved, less welcoming, than other towns we've visited. No one greets us on the street and the old people stare as we walk by, noting we are strangers. The pottery shops are fantastic with a huge variety of sizes, shapes and colors at very reasonable prices. On the sidewalks outside the shops there are huge planters and fountains for sale; picnic tables, barbecues and benches, cast in white concrete. There are concrete figurines also, the most popular motifs being snow white and the seven dwarfs, frogs, eagles, pine cones, boots, sheep, naked women, little boys tinkling and maidens carrying jugs. Wildly popular, hardly a house can be found on the entire coast without at least one of these figurines on the fence post or in the garden. At some homes, people have gone wild and have twenty or thirty small replicas of Sleepy, Dopey and Grumpy scattered around the garden.

Every inch of the pottery shop floors, walls and ceilings are covered with pottery. There are glazed ceramic plates, wall lamps and hanging lamps, fountains and tiles in bright colors. I walk gingerly through the aisles, careful not to bump into anything and bring the stacks crashing down around me. Pottery and planters are stacked in row after row, at first a few inches in diameter until, in the lot at the back of the shop, they are as tall as I and large enough to bathe in. I have a hard time choosing but finally select three pots with flowers hand painted in green, blue and yellow. They will hold bright red and pink geraniums for our front porch.

We drive back to *Vidreres* to do some grocery shopping and drop off some mail for Marta. We notice that our back fender has two new dents above the wheel. Dennis is upset, "One day, ONE BLOODY DAY to get dented in this country." We expected that it would happen eventually but we can't believe it happened so fast. Marta tells us, "Don't be upset, it was inevitable." Marta's house is on a narrow cobblestone street and she has to park her car on the street outside. Her mirror has been smashed twice so she knows what it feels like. She tries to comfort us. "You have to just accept it. It's like the French," she says, "when they invite someone to dinner; they spread a clean white tablecloth on the table then throw a glass of red wine on it. They know stains are inevitable and this way none of the guests feel bad when they spill."

We drive to *Lloret* to go to the library and get some photocopies made. It's a Tuesday in the middle of November and everything is closed. We don't listen to TV or radio or read newspapers and we can hardly speak to our neighbors so we had no idea that it was a holiday. It makes us realize how isolated we are. The only place with any activity is the city square. It's a science fair of some kind, a little Exploratorium. There are home made contraptions for the children to play with. It looks as though old people have taken junk from their garages and made games for the children. There is a silhouette of a chicken made from hoses and pipe hoisted up on a pole. By spinning a wheel, the chicken drops a wooden egg that's attached to a kind of bungee cord. The children try to catch the egg with a pair of tongs. They are squealing and laughing and an old man is trying to help them. Another contraption's made of an old wire bedspring with a funnel in the center. The children are given a tire jack with a golf ball glued to the end and they hit the springs from the bottom and try to make a tennis ball jump into the funnel. Another man has made a two-railed spiral, like a double helix, out of old bicycle wheels and balanced the whole thing on a pole so it can be tilted back and forth. The children are trying to roll a ball from the top to bottom by controlling the tilt. This one is difficult, they have to try to slow the ball down to be successful and it simply goes against their nature to make it go slow-they want it to go fast. I love seeing the children and old people interacting. Everything is free. No one here is out to make money and the children are actually sharing with each other and not fighting. We watch one frustrated dad as he tries to teach a small child how to bounce a wooden egg into a cup. The egg is balanced on a springboard so gently tapping the board with a hammer makes it bounce into the cup. The little girl keeps bashing the egg as soon as he puts the hammer in her hand. Her dad keeps shaking his head and showing her what she is supposed to do but she just can't resist bashing that egg.

Conversation Class without Conversation

We have a Spanish conversation class on Fridays but the professor loves to talk and we students hardly get a word in. I don't mind because I find the professor fascinating.

She tells us about the autonomous regions of Spain and the different languages and dialects of the country. She used to teach in public school and tells us about children who use Catalan in the classroom and then switch to *Castellano* as soon as they walk out the door. She explains that living with these two languages is just a fact in this area, like it or not.

She tells us about the oppressive years under Franco and how Spain changed after his death (too fast for most people). She explains how the Catholic Church dominated education and the life here, even choosing the name of your child. If it was born on a Saints day, it was baptized with the name of that Saint whether you wanted it or not. She explains that women were not allowed to smoke outside the home, smoke inside the home yes, but only whores smoked in public. To this day, if her mother-in-law sees a woman smoking on the street she will point and say "*una mujer perdida*", a lost woman. But young people don't have the same attitude. They dress how they want and smoke. Young women are the worst. The percent that smoke is so high the government is worried about it and has started education classes in the schools.

She explains that Franco, unwilling to have any opposition in the country, hunted all the intelligentsia. They either fled into exile or died. It has taken decades for Spain to recover, to have art, literature, films, science and research again.

There's an unusual black market of seamstresses here, uneducated women who can't find jobs outside the home, who earn a living by hemming pants. *Pantalones*, trousers are sold in one length only, long. In general, the Spanish are quite short people[1]. This has lead to employment for women who would other-wise be quite desperate. "Look for the signs in the windows that say *hacemos arreglos*, we do alterations."

She tells us that the Spanish have a "decided shape." Women who have raised a family and reach a certain age acquire it. She uses her hands to demonstrate, "like small refrigerators." We can see this is true. Walk the city streets and you will see short square women in shapeless paisley housedresses lumbering through the city streets hauling bags of groceries or pulling shopping carts. I think it applies to the men too. Wiry and lithe in youth, by middle age they too develop round torsos, like small wine barrels.

Most Spanish don't eat breakfast at home. The get up and are out the door in fifteen minutes. They go to work or school then an hour or so later they go out to the bakery for a pastry and a coffee. Some go to the bar for a *bocadillo*, a sand-wich, and a shot of strong alcohol. A few years ago it was not unusual to go into a post office or a bank and every window would be closed, all the employees were eating breakfast. Since Spain joined the EU this has changed, they have to take turns now so at least one person is in the office but they still go eat something during work hours.

She tells us about her vacation riding a burro in the wild mountains of *Andalucía*. She describes that unspoiled wilderness, the clear cold nights and the quiet, unhurried life of the locals. She tells us about another vacation to the *Parc Natural Delta de l'Ebre*, a bird habitat on the southern coast of Catalunya. It's an unspoiled little known place where birds from Northern Europe and even pink flamingoes, spend their winters.

She talks of the Spanish love of cured ham. How the pigs are raised and cared for as carefully as possible, then the meat is treated with tender loving care, salted and cured in the open air in the mountains. She explains how the meat is rated and stamped with regional codes, like fine wine, the finest quality having a JJJJ rating from the pueblo *Jabugo*. Then for the Muslims in the class, about the fine cured meats made from sheep.

She explains about the Spanish love of going on strike. Businesses and public transportation are often closed down by strikes. Sometimes it seems like people just don't want to work. She tells us of the use of *puente*, bridge. That if a festival

---

1. At five foot three inches, I'm taller than almost everybody I meet in Spain, women and men. What a huge contrast to Norway where I was shorter than EVERYONE. I was too short to trigger the automated door. I had to wave my hand in the air to open them. I had to go to the children's department to find ski clothes in my size and stand on a box at the immigration office to see over the desk.

falls on a Tuesday then the preceding Monday is automatically a holiday. If the holiday is on Thursday, then Friday is *puente*.

I love this conversation class. I'm not getting much practice with Spanish but I'm grateful for this teacher. There's so much to learn about this country, so much to learn about living here.

Marta and Carlos

Marta threw Carlos out of the house. She packed up all his clothes and put them outside in the street. Carlos has moved in with his mother in *Blanes*. Carlos and Marta are explaining what has happened over lunch at a vegetarian restaurant in the coastal town of *Callela*.

"I don't know why. I normally don't react, but this time I just got so fed up with him always going to bars and drinking, that I just overreacted."

I'm surprised when Carlos says, "I wanted her to do it; I'm an egoist."

Marta corrects his English. "You mean to say you are selfish."

"Yes, yes I am selfish," he agrees.

The waiter comes to take our order. I can't understand one word of the menu. I think it is in Catalan, not Spanish. At least I hope my Spanish is not that bad. Marta translates for us and we order. The restaurant sits a block away from the ocean on a narrow tourist street near the old town church. It is one of a long row of two story houses with a small private garden/kitchen in the back. The dining area is long and narrow and barely two tables wide with a wooden bar dividing the room in the middle. The walls are old, raw stone and there are paper lamps with patterns of dried leaves hanging above the tables. The feel is organic, earthy, comfortable.

Marta explains, "I shouldn't have done it. It wasn't the right thing to do. Normally I don't react. I treat what he says as a joke. If he says that he wants to be alone, that doesn't want girlfriends, then I tell him, 'of course you don't want girlfriends, you have me.' If he says he wants his freedom then I say, 'I didn't pay for you, you are free.' But something happened this time, I just took it wrong and packed up all his things."

Carlos says, "I love Marta, she is my friend. I do good things when I am with her. But I have this dark in my mind. I don't want to see it sometimes but it is there. I think I have to be alone to look at this dark side."

Dennis and I agree, we also have dark sides to our mind and relationships are certainly not easy but we have no advice to give them. Carlos leaves tomorrow to take a job in Andorra for the winter season. The winter tourists come from all over Spain and Europe to ski and to buy duty free goods. Carlos doesn't usually work during the winter season, he says summers are enough and he can use the winter to read and write and garden. "Why should I work so hard?" he says. "I am not alive so I can work more, at least I don't believe it."

Our first course arrives. I have ordered wonderful roasted winter vegetables with a pesto sauce. The others have a Thai rice salad with roasted Portobello mushrooms. We talk about Carlos's childhood. His mother was very dominating. He tells us that she shared all her worries about her business and love life with him, even when he was a small child. He says he was so overwhelmed he could sometimes not even speak. It wasn't until he turned 18 that he finally was able to break away and do something she did not approve of. "I loved a girl my mother did not like," he tells us. She was so upset that she lay on the sofa for three days and did not eat and did not speak to anyone. My brothers and sisters told me I was killing her but I just told them, "she is killing herself." After three days she gave up and I stayed with my girlfriend. After that she accepted that I sometimes have my own life. She was very unhappy with me. I went wild, took drugs, got angry and in fights but she could not stop me. Now we are friends again. Of course she still tries to tell me what to do, but I do what I want now.

Marta has to leave the table since the kids are getting restless and need to go outside. Carlos tells us when she is gone that he has really tried to tell Marta from the beginning that he did not want a girlfriend. "She was my teacher, and I told her, I don't want a girlfriend. She just said, 'of course you don't, kiss me!' Now I tell her I am not a good father for her children and she tells me I am; but I don't want to be, I am not ready for it. When she threw me out my mother was happy, Marta is a lot older than me. 'Now you can find a younger girlfriend and have children' she told me. "I don't want a younger girlfriend, I don't want children. I don't want to hurt Marta."

I feel so sorry. If he really feels this way, how can they stay together? Marta has children. She has no choice about being a mother. I think we all looked depressed when Marta returns with the kids. She immediately changes the subject and we discuss a book she is reading by a French philosopher that has really changed her view of the world. We tell her about an article we read by an expert on polygraphs. He had done an experiment where he got an electrochemical response from a plant when he threatened it. Later, after working with plants, bacteria, and eggs, he started to wonder how human cells would react. He used scrapings from the roof of a person's mouth and found out that cells outside the body still react to the emotions you feel, even though you may be miles away. This simple article changed my view of the world. Perhaps there is a connectedness between living things that we have no conscious knowledge of.

We sit quietly for a few minutes. I am thinking that our cells are probably reacting at this very minute to this day and to the troubles in the air. So ends our lunch and we walk with Carlos and Marta to their car. I am wondering if we will ever see them again together.

Pig Jowls and Tripe

We've fallen in love with *menu del dia,* a set menu lunch including wine for a very reasonable 7.00-10.00 Euro. They serve it at nearly every restaurant in the area. It can be a hit or miss affair. The food quality varies with the restaurant and so does the wine. We have occasionally been disappointed in the quality but usually we're pleasantly satisfied. We have learned to stay away from the coastal towns and eat inland. The small town of *Vidreres* has some very good restaurants with reasonable prices. Often we can't understand the menus because they are in Catalan. We often have to guess what we are ordering. There have been a few surprises. Dennis ordered a meat dish one day called *galtas* and even after eating the whole plateful, he simply could not identify which kind of meat it was. We finally asked the waiter and found out that it was the jowls of a pig. I'm reminded of the Norwegian dish *smalahode* (a sheep head). Lovers of the dish say that the jowls are the best part. I find this hard to believe as its one part of a sheep that never stops moving its whole life. Dennis confirms their statement though, pigs seem to eat constantly too and yet the *galtas* were very good.

At a restaurant in *Blanes* I asked the waitress about *callos* but she couldn't really explain what it was. She said it was the house specialty and very good so we both ordered it. Unfortunately, it turned out to be tripe. I'm usually brave about trying new foods but tripe has the texture of mushy squid. Hoping the dish had potatoes or mushrooms in it I tried several bites. Every bite had the same disgusting texture. I left my meal untouched. Dennis agreed with me but ate his whole plate anyway. He said later that he didn't like it but was too embarrassed to leave both of our meals untouched. I wrote down the word *callos* and carry it in my purse just to be sure I never order it again.

Our favorite restaurant is behind a small bar in *Vidreres*. We've been there three times and the waitress has stopped showing us the menu. Instead she puts her arms around our shoulders and recites the *menu del dia* in a mixture of Catalan and *Castellano*. There's always a fresh green salad with vinegar and olive oil, a first course of soup, vegetables, *paella*, or *fideus*, a dish similar to *paella* but made with tiny pasta instead of rice. The main course is fish or meat grilled or served in a stew. Then either ice cream, yogurt, fresh fruit or *crema catalana* for dessert. We always opt for the *crema catalana,* a custard dish with a burned sugar crust, because at this restaurant it is done to perfection.

We discovered *menu del dia* by accident. When we entered a restaurant, they asked, "*Menu?*" I assumed it meant, "Do you want to see a menu?" The actual question was, "Do you want *menu del dia?*" We've made the mistake twice now and we're happy we did.

We love taking a walk after a big lunch and wander around town or stroll the beach. During the lunch hours the promenade at the beach in *Lloret de Mar* is full of people. I love the way they stroll. I have never seen people move so slowly. Arms linked and chatting they have no goal. They just enjoy the sun and each other's company. I've never lived in a place where people just meander. Even cross country skiing in Norway, which is done for pure pleasure, is done with a purpose; to reach that lake or this cabin or to finish a certain track. Here people don't have to go anywhere, don't have to be anywhere. They have forgotten the clock.

SOS Lloret

A big, gray German Shepard terrorized one of our cats. She refuses to stay inside the fence where the dogs can't get her. She was sunning herself on a rock in the empty lot next door and was taken by surprise. We don't know if she's twisted her back but she can hardly walk. There is blood on her tail but we can't find a wound. I call the vet in *Lloret de Mar*. We saw his office the first day we were there. He advertised 'English Spoken' so I copied down his number from a sign outside his office. I get his answering machine when I try to call. The message is first in Spanish, then in German but the vet picks up the phone interrupting the message. I explain the problem and he tells us we can bring our cat right in.

His office is empty when we arrive and the doctor greets us. He is a handsome, thin man with short black hair, a thin black mustache and creamy brown skin. He's wearing a knee length, white lab coat over blue jeans. He asks if we are the British people who called. Yes, we called but we are American. He asks, "Have we have been living in *Lloret* long? Why are we here? Do we like it?" We explain that we have just arrived and are living in an *urbanización* in the mountains about ten minutes from *Lloret* but that we are looking for a home to buy.

While he examines Murphy, I tell him his English is excellent. He says that it's normal for doctors to know English because it's required at school. "Of course some people are more interested in it than others. I like it."

He can't find any injury on Murphy and thinks she is just sore. Where the blood came from is a mystery, maybe from the dog? "Give her a few days and if she is not better bring her back." He checks her for fleas and ticks then gives us some medicine. "She doesn't have them right now but you should use this because eventually she will get them."

When we are leaving, I see a paper on the counter with lots of signatures on it. The heading reads SOS *LLoret*. I've seen posters up around town with this heading so I ask him what it is about. "It's a group of people who think they are doing too much building in *Lloret*. If they keep going, soon *Lloret* will be a suburb of Barcelona."

"You're kidding?" I ask, surprised.

"Well yes and no. It could happen. Barcelona is swallowing all the towns around it and reaching further and further away. Here in *Lloret* they are building with no controls. It's madness. Last year they built a big hotel on the nicest beach. It was a beach that was for the locals, tourist too, but mostly local people, and they just took it. In the mountains just a few kilometers from here there is a place called *Mont Lloret*. They want to develop it, to put in 900 more homes. We don't want them to do it. There are already problems with water in the summers and in the winter the power always goes out. Also, there are just two small, narrow roads going up the hill to the area. Can you imagine all the traffic? SOS *Lloret* is trying to stop it."

We're shocked. *Mont Lloret* is only two streets away from our house. Does Marta know? We exclaim, "Wow, they will really ruin that area. We go walking there sometimes and it's beautiful, just *bosque* and lots of wildlife."

He tells us, "I hate the way they build here. They remove every single plant. They leave nothing but dirt. I read this book about American architects. I can't believe it. Even fifty years ago they build homes that live side by side with the trees and plants. If you try to see the house from the road, you can hardly see it. Here they take everything away, cover it with concrete. Then someone buys it, puts a few plants in pots, sits on their concrete veranda and says they are living in the country. I think we can learn a lot from America but if we don't learn after fifty years, then when will we?"

Dennis tells him, "It does seem like they are building like crazy. But I guess we are part of the problem too. We are looking for a home to buy. It's like saying, 'We can come in but you should lock the door behind us.'"

The vet asks us, "What do you do? I hope you have a lot of money. It's very expensive here."

I shake my head, "Well, I am planning to teach English and we don't have a lot of money. We like *Girona* so much we decided to look near there first. That's too expensive so we are looking around here. We've gone inland and there are some nice towns there, like *Santa Coloma* and *Arbucies*. We like *Arbucies* quite a lot."

"That's where all the rich people in Barcelona go for vacation. Guess who is moving to *Arbucies?*" he adds.

"Who?"

"Guess."

I try to think of a famous Spanish person and can only come up with one name, "Antonio Banderas?"

"No, Tina Turner. I just read in the paper that she visited there and loved it. She is going to build a house there."

"Oh no, that means the prices will really go up."

"Yes probably," he agrees.

We haven't even started looking yet and we are already disappointed. "Maybe we will have to look in another part of Spain. Maybe *Huesca*."

"They would love it if you moved to *Huesca*. Many people are leaving there. Do you have children? If you have five children then we have this funny law in Spain that there has to be school. You could move to a small town and start a school and teach English."

"No, no we don't have children and I'm not interested in teaching them. I want to work with adults."

"Maybe you can move to *Garroxta*. It's in the north. It's cheaper up there and it's very beautiful. They are going to build a high-speed train to France too. In a few years, you will be able to live in *Figueres* and work in Barcelona. They are already building like crazy in *Figueres* because of it."

"More building?"

"Yes. That's why I belong to SOS *Lloret*."

Enigma

The European Commission is puzzled about why Spaniards live so long. I've just read about a study on health, aging and retirement in Europe which states that Spaniards are the most overweight and depressed people in Europe and yet they live the longest. A huge percent of people over the age of sixty-five are depressed. By the time Spaniards reach the age of fifty most are overweight and sedentary. Even so they have one of the lowest rates of heart disease in Europe. This used to be blamed on the Mediterranean diet but the study also showed that this diet was no longer being followed. People eat fatter foods, smoke and drink more and no longer exercise. When they do walk, they walk more slowly than Northern Europeans. Despite all the bad habits, they are at the top of the list in life expectancy in Europe. Perhaps the answer lies in family? Spaniards rank the highest in having contact with family. Half of the people over the age of fifty say they see their children everyday. One third of people over sixty-five say they spend their day with small children. Perhaps the reason is the quality of life that Dennis and I have discovered here. The Spanish have something that we cannot put our finger on, something elusive, that we find difficult to describe. It's an attitude, a mood, perhaps temperament that makes life here just a little more relaxed, a little slower, a little sweeter.

This place is a strange mix of technology and third world. The motorway has electronic signs posting current gasoline prices, information about opening times for restaurants and truck stops yet we see men in overalls painting the dotted lines on the highway by hand; with a bucket and brush. They have modern bulldozers, backhoes and drills for land development, but we still see construction workers tearing apart concrete with a hammer and chisel. They have modern, heated and cooled greenhouses then haul the produce to market with a horse and cart. The post office has electronic doors and stamp dispensers but the postmen have to search through plastic boxes and stacks of letters bound with rubber bands to fetch your mail.

I get the feeling that human labor is cheap and expendable. No one EVER wears safety equipment. We saw one man shaving bricks with a handheld power saw wearing no gloves, no coveralls, no earmuffs, nor protective glasses. He had to work with his head turned away and eyes closed because of the flying dust.

Labor may be cheap but they go at it with heart. We often hear construction workers and garbage men singing as they work, sometimes with a radio blaring but also just belted *acappella*. They are polite and greet passers by with *buenas* or *hola* and I've never heard catcalls. They are not, however, embarrassed to silently ogle women and do it with gusto.

They've started construction on a house next door. The workers arrive about 8:00 in the morning bringing equipment and tools. About a half hour later, they all speed off to have breakfast at the restaurant at the entrance of our *urbanización*. They return around 9:00 and begin the workday. They take their long Spanish lunch at 2:00 and return around 3:30 to continue until dark, usually around 8:00 in the evening. There is always a radio blaring at full volume. They turn down the radio immediately when I ask but it slowly creeps up in volume as the day progresses and different men come and go. These men work seven days a week, although Sunday seems to have slightly shorter work hours. The gate to our driveway is close to the property line and they park in front of it everyday blocking our exit. We have Spanish classes on weekday mornings so before we leave Dennis has to go out to ask them to move their trucks. We're curious to see how many days it will take them to stop blocking the gate. Tomorrow will be day fifteen…

I'm reading an interesting book about contemporary Spain[1]. I learn that there are fiercely independent regions of Spain with their own language and culture. For rare, short periods of history the regions have been united, the latest being under the dictatorship of Franco. But most of the regions have always resisted (internally or externally) these unions. The Basque region with its ETA terrorists is well known even outside of Spain. I learn that other regions want independence from Spain just as fiercely but are obtaining it by peaceful political tactics. *Catalunya* has been very successful at this and the Catalan language, banned under Franco, has flourished in the years since his death. Catalan is not a dialect, but its own language which sounds like a mix of Spanish, French and Italian. It causes enormous difficulties for us. We are struggling with Spanish, which is difficult enough, but we should really be learning both languages simultaneously. Most public information; signs, bulletins, menus and government forms are written in Catalan. I can't read more than a few words. I know that if we remain in

---

1.   John Hooper, *The New Spaniards*

Catalunya that we will have to learn yet another language but my brain is overloaded right now with Spanish.

I'm surprised to learn that Spain is such a young democracy. Franco died without an heir. After his death in 1975 the country precariously swayed between military dictatorship, monarchy and democracy. Amazingly enough King Juan Carlos, Franco's appointed successor, threw his weight behind democracy and Spain had its first election in 1976. It adopted its first unilateral constitution in late 1978. Being ignorant of Spain's history before coming here, I'm shocked to learn that the country has been a democracy for only 26 years. I've always considered the United States a young democracy but it's a granddad compared to Spain. I'm amazed at how the country, completely frozen in time and isolated from Europe during Franco's era, has evolved into a European nation on par with France or Germany.

I understand now why Spaniards don't know English. Spain was isolated from Europe and ostracized by America during Franco's regime. While other countries in Europe embraced English as a business and education language, in Spain it simply wasn't used. It's been changing since Spain joined the European Union in the early 1990's but they still lag far behind the rest of Europe in their English ability. The imported British and American TV shows are dubbed into Spanish or regional languages. Now, the demand for English is enormous. That's part of the reason it's easy to find a job teaching English here. When I took my teacher certification most of my fellow students were young, American graduates looking for a way to live and work in Spain for a year or two. Most of them, not allowed to work legally, had no trouble finding jobs.

Christmas and "Shit! Uncle"

The temperature has dropped. The high today is only 10 C° (about 35 F°) and it's almost Christmas. We almost resent having to put on a coat to go for a walk. It's cloudy with periods of sun, but the sun does not warm. In the neighborhood, we see a few Christmas decorations, most seem like an afterthought, just some lights thrown on one of the trees in the yard. A few homes have makeshift Christmas trees; sticks placed in buckets and decorated with bulbs and tinsel. Some people have put wreaths on their doors and windows. Then I remember that most of these homes are vacation properties. People probably decorate their homes in the city. In town there are a few decorations hanging in the streets and some Christmas trees standing in big clay pots on the streets. Otherwise, we have not noticed too much Christmas rush or any extra shopping. Only the post office seems to have a long, slow queue but since we have never been there before this may be normal.

Walking near our house we are both startled by the loud gobble of a turkey! We can see four bright blue heads sticking up over a concrete fence. We are so surprised by their color that we wonder if they are real until we see their heads bob and they start to gobble again. Such a strange sound. Dennis says that if he had painted his Thanksgiving turkey with a blue head like that in grade school, his teacher would have corrected him saying; "turkeys don't have blue heads!"

A stray dog joins us for our walk. We have learned not to pet these animals or they will follow us home. This one must belong to someone, he looks healthy and he's beautiful, like a light brown wolf with blue gray eyes. Suddenly, up ahead; a chicken runs across the road and the dog darts after him. "Might be the last day for that chicken," Dennis comments. I'm nervous for the bird as we watch but at the last minute, it takes to flight squawking and lands in a nearby orange tree. The dog leaps into the air, missing by a long shot but the bird is frightened and awkwardly jumps to another branch, almost falling. If it would just stay put it would be OK. I remember a story a guide told us walking through a jungle in Nepal. The monkeys are safe high up in the treetops. When a tiger comes through the jungle, the monkeys get so frightened that they jump up and down, fall out of the trees and the tiger eats them. I wonder how often we act in fear and do exactly the wrong thing. We would like to help the chicken but we are not willing to come between a strange wolf dog and potential dinner. We leave the chicken in the tree with the dog sitting below. At the top of the hill we suddenly hear loud squawking and turn to look but can't see what has happened.

At the craft market in *Lloret* we see the wildly popular miniature nativity scenes for sale. One person is selling moss collected from the forest, used in the nativity scenes. Other stalls have figurines; baby Jesus, Mary, Joseph, shepherds, sheep and cows in all sizes and colors. We are shocked to see one display that has nothing but small figurines of boys, with their pants pulled down around their knees squatting over a pile of shit. It must be some kind of joke. Another man is selling a log with a small Santa hat and a smiley face painted on the end, propped up on a three cornered stand. I've never seen these before and assume they are Yule logs. The next day in Spanish class we ask about the logs and our Spanish teacher explains. Children give food to the log during December, oranges, apples or yogurt. On Christmas Eve the log gives them presents in return. It used to give chocolate or candy but now it is bicycles and computers. Can this really be? A log that gives gifts? The tradition seems so pagan to me, so strange in a predominantly Catholic country.

On December 22 Spain comes to a virtual standstill for *El Gordo*, the Fat One; the biggest lottery of the year, with prizes in the hundreds of millions of euro. Winners are announced on television, the numbers are sung out loudly by children of all ages until the big jackpot is finally revealed. Individual lottery tickets are very expensive so people buy parts of tickets. Often entire villages join together to buy a lucky number so when the big win finally comes, everyone in town gets a share. This year we watch the winners, an entire village in *Jaen* gathers in the local bar and cracks bottle after bottle of champagne to celebrate. Even the children are there, grinning from ear to ear. At the end of the broadcast, they show the bitterest man in Spain. He bought an entire ticket all to himself and was one digit away from winning the jackpot.

Christmas Eve appears to be a normal day. The construction workers put in a full day and the shops are open as usual. Everything will be closed tomorrow, at least in the morning. A few restaurants are serving a Christmas *menu del dia*. The prices are much higher than the normal *menu*, ranging from 20 to 100 Euro per person. The temperature has dropped even more. We had a hard frost during the night that left a layer of ice on the windshield of our car. The roads are slippery in places. We are doing volunteer work at a nearby meditation center, painting and cleaning. We work hard the whole day, trying to prepare the center for a course that will be starting just after Christmas. We're exhausted as we arrive home on

Christmas Eve. We don't feel like going out and I certainly don't feel like cooking. I reheat some leftover pinto beans while Dennis builds a fire. Soon the fire is toasty warm so we bring in the lawn chairs from the patio and sit right in front of it. Perhaps next year we will have a real Christmas dinner but this year we sit with our bowls of beans, wishing each other merry Christmas. Our first Christmas in Spain.

We visit Marta for lunch on Christmas day. She has cleared one shelf on a bookcase for a Nativity scene. We stand close to admire it and are surprised to see one of those figurines of the little boy taking a dump. When we ask about it she laughs; "My mother was shocked, I mean really SHOCKED when she first saw it, but now she accepts it and even smiles when she sees it. It's a Catalan thing. Every nativity scene has to have its *cacanen*; it's shitting boy."

"Isn't it kind of sacrilegious?" I ask.

"It seems that way at first but when you think about it, it's just reality. Jesus being born, heaven came to earth, but at the same time, life goes on. Someone, somewhere, still had to do what humans have to do. I really like this about the Catalan people, they are very earthy."

Later Marta brings out a Yule log like the ones we saw at the market. I comment on how pagan this tradition seems. It turns out that our Spanish teacher has given us the polite version of the tradition. Marta is setting the table with plates and cups and we get the story in bits and pieces as she walks back and forth to the kitchen. She explains, "In Catalan the log is called a *Cacatio*. It's an imperative. It means 'Shit! Uncle.' In December the children leave it food. Someone has to remove the food every night because the children all check to see if it has been 'eaten'. You know, if the log doesn't eat, it can't shit so they make sure. On Christmas Eve, the children have to sing a song to the log. It's covered with a big cloth. Someone called a *tio* (an uncle) hides under the cloth so the children can see that something begins to move. They have to leave the room for a few minutes and when they return the log has literally shat presents. It's a strong tradition here in *Catalunya*. Just go to *Vidreres* or one of the small *pueblos* on Christmas Eve and you will see it. All the children go there and the *ayuntamiento* buys gifts for them and gives them away through the *cacatio*. You have to understand, this is strictly Catalan. It wouldn't happen in other parts of Spain. It would upset the Spanish *delicadeza*."

Dennis and I look at each other and smile. I know we are thinking the same thing. There seems to be a lot of excrement involved in the Catalan Christmas.

A few days after Christmas, the temperatures are still low during the day and near freezing at night. I don't understand it but I already see signs of spring. The grapevine in the garden has a few tender young shoots. The strawberries have started to flower and I can see clover seeds beginning to sprout. It seems so strange Carlos's sweet peppers are still producing from last year, and the new season is starting.

We have read that rather than Christmas, the big celebration in Spain is on Jan 6, *Dia de los Reyes Magos*, Three Kings Day. The Kings replace our traditional Santa Claus. Children even write to ask them for presents. They represent the three *Magi* who brought gifts to the baby Jesus. On the *costas* the Kings and their entourage usually arrive by boat from the sea. We decide to go to *Lloret* and watch the celebrations. It's been a warm day but the temperature is dropping with the sun. As we walk toward the beach there are children everywhere bundled in coats and knit hats. They are carrying lanterns on the end of sticks and waving them in the air. There's music blaring out of raspy speakers at the town hall. The tall Christmas tree in the square is lit up with a swirl of white lights. It seems incongruous to have this tall pine tree standing in front of a long line of palm trees. Barriers have been put up to block off traffic from the beach road. It's lined with people of all ages. The atmosphere is electric. It's contagious and we can't stand still so we walk back and forth along the beach. When darkness falls the church bells start ringing and we see police lights flashing at the end of the street. The crowd presses toward the lights and there are the kings! Men standing atop large floats, dressed in long flowing robes, white beards and crowns. They zing candy at us, throwing so hard it shatters as it hits the ground. The children scramble to grab every piece. They slowly parade down the street followed by a large truck filled with gifts, hundreds of boxes wrapped in Christmas paper with ribbons and bows. We find out later that this is only symbolic; the boxes are empty, the children will get their gifts at home. At the city square, someone has built thrones, one for each king. I can see that the black king is shoe polish black, his white neck glows from under his fake beard. There's a short speech by the mayor of the city. We understand little because it's in Catalan, until he tells everyone: *Canta!* Sing! After the song, the crowd presses toward the thrones. The smallest children are riding on their parent's shoulders. Then the kings sit at their thrones and hand out little bags of candy to the children as they file past. The older children are confident and proudly march up on their own but some of the younger ones are overwhelmed; many have to be led by hand to the kings. They are anxious to go home where they will find the presents they have asked for.

We walk back toward the car after the ceremonies and decide to stop in a bar or cafe to have a drink before we head home. The cafes are all full of people still excited from the evening. The one we select is crowded two or three people deep at the bar. We have to press between the crowds to order. Not everyone is full of Christmas cheer; the bartender frazzled and overworked scowls and yells the price to us as she brings our wine.

Singing at the Fish Market, Half a Piglet, Olives and Yogurt

Other than produce, we have started to do our grocery shopping at the Spanish food chain *Mercadona*. The prices are 20-50% less than in any other food store. Unlike other businesses, the grocery stores are open all day. It's fun and challenging but often frustrating to shop when we can't read. The largest sections here are the fresh fish, meat and alcohol.

The selection of fish is amazing and the prices very cheap. We don't know the names of fish in Spanish and can't identify most of them. On Saturdays the fish section is so busy you have to take a number and wait in line. I am waiting in the queue just after Christmas and the women are singing out numbers and everyone is laughing. At first, I don't understand what is going on, then I realized they are imitating the children who sing out the numbers for *El Gordo*. What a contrast to Norway. The people there are so reserved. I can imagine a Norwegian singing at the fish market only on two conditions: 1) they are half drunk or 2) they are dead drunk.

There is a large variety of frozen fish and we see Norwegian salmon frozen and smoked. The seafood rice specialty, *Paella*, traditionally from Valencia, is very popular here with a large variety of prepackaged shellfish and vegetable mixes for sale. There are special short grain *paella* rice, broths, spices and colorings that even merit their own rack in the aisle.

The meat section is difficult for me to stomach, as they tend to leave the skinned heads on some of the animals; rabbits, ducks, lamb. For Christmas they had baby pigs, about the size of a turkey, sliced in half lengthwise and sold like a package of chicken or hamburger; head tail, hoofs and all. They sell every part of the animal here. There's a package of chicken feet, little boxes of kidneys and livers and I've even see ears for sale. There is a large selection of dried salted meats like the Norwegian *spekemat* and the much loved cured ham.

The alcohol section is enormous and includes beer, wine and hard liquors. The wines vary in price; local *bodegas* (wine cellars) bottles cost a few euros with the exclusive aged reserves from *La Rioja* selling for much, much more. *Bodega's* wines can range from quite good to downright vile. Almost every town we've visited has their own *bodegas* and their wines are sold tapped from large barrels into whatever container you have brought along—an old plastic water jug, rinsed out wine bottle, even ice tea glasses. There are always plastic jugs for sale in case you don't have one. These large barrels are found in the most unusual places. A restaurant at the entrance to our *urbanización* has a small back room where you can buy wine from the barrel. Even the pet food shop in *Lloret de Mar* has two large barrels sitting between the sacks of dog food and kitty litter.

Mercadona (and all the other grocery stores) have an enormous variety of olives. We soon discover that they are the appetizers of choice. Normally after placing your order at a restaurant, you are given a small plate of olives, while you wait for your first course. There is also a huge selection of canned fish. Sardines and mussels are available in every kind of sauce, from simple olive oil to spicy chile, tomato, vinaigrette, lemon, herbs, and garlic.

It's difficult to find sour cream or kefir but they have an enormous selection of yogurts in flavors I've never seen like lemon, papaya and kiwi. The Spanish dessert *flan* and the Catalan favorite *crema catalana* are sold in a large variety of pre-packaged versions. The milk and cream is sold in cartons, not bottles and at room temperature. Something bothers me about buying milk that can sit on the shelf un-refrigerated for months without spoiling. What have they done to the milk to make it last indefinitely?

Although the tap water here is supposed to be safe, nearly everyone buys water for drinking. Our tap water smells like chlorine so we also buy purified water at a cheap thirty *centimos* per liter.

The produce section is large and the vegetables very cheap compared to Norwegian prices. The grocery stores here, like Norway tend to use a lot of plastic and prepackaging which I find disappointing. Not only does it generate more trash, and contaminate the produce with petrochemical emissions, we simply like to smell and feel what we are buying. We have to learn to weigh our own produce and tag it ourselves as they rarely have scales at the registers. We have made this mistake twice now irritating the checkout clerk and pissing off the people in the queue behind us.

The local street markets are my favorite places to buy fruit and vegetables. The selection of fruit and vegetables is larger, the prices cheaper and the quality is better than the grocery stores. It's difficult to find parking in the cities or pueblos. The streets are narrow, cobblestone often blocked by delivery vans or construction vehicles so we park on the outskirts and walk in. I have to remind myself that I will have to carry everything I buy a long way back to the car. When I'm by myself I debate buying wine or juice or even a bag of potatoes. Do I really want it bad enough to carry it one or two kilometers? When Dennis is with me he becomes my beast of burden. I'm surprised but he rarely complains about this. Only once he put his foot down when I was eyeing a large watermelon. The local women own canvas shopping bags on wheels. They load them up and pull them bouncing along the cobblestones or through the dirt.

Some vendors like to select the produce for you, rather than letting you grab your own, but they also seem to be careful to select good quality. Others let you fill your own bags and simply weigh and price it for you. I've learned to ask permission before I touch the vegetables with a simple "*puedo?*" Can I? At these markets, there are also a wide variety of spices, kitchenware, household goods, meats, cheeses, and clothing. The atmosphere is festive even on these cold winter mornings. I am still wary of pickpockets. My husband was pick pocketed once, left with no money, no wallet and an overwhelming sense of helplessness and anger. That is enough to make you cautious even in the quiet of the winter in Costa Brava.

I puzzle over the places things are sold. Why is paint sold together with perfume? Why is wine sold at the pet food store? Why do you buy stamps at the tobacco shop? Why can you open a bank account at the post office? There must be some historical reasons for these strange groupings but I don't know what they are.

We learn that if a restaurant or shop is small you should say a greeting "*buenas*" when you enter and "*hasta luego*" or the Catalan "*Déo*"[1] when you leave. Otherwise, you are considered rude (or a foreigner). If the shop is large, you greet the clerk when you check out. We often forget and have to remind ourselves to do it the next time.

As we drive between the local towns, we see factories and shops lining the highway. I don't have a clue what most of these are and it makes me feel strangely unsettled. It adds to my feeling of displacement. When I drove in America or Norway I instinctively knew what the businesses were. Some places are obvious, like the construction supply and the garden shop but what do they sale at *Foc du LLar*? At *Cecam*? What do they make at the *Gel* factory? What do they sell at *Liberto Factory Store*? What are *Rétols*? What do the people do who work in these places? Run a cash register? Drive a truck? Work on a computer? I don't have a clue. I would like to stop, stick my head in the door and find out but I don't.

---

1.   Short for "Adéu", goodbye

New Year and Shin Chan

Marta invites me over for lunch on New Year's Day. Dennis is away on a meditation course so, tired of being alone, I am grateful for the invitation. Carlos is in Andorra working and Marta's mother is visiting for Christmas. Her mother is a small stately woman. The first thing she asks is if I speak French or German. Unfortunately I don't. Marta explains that I know very little Spanish. Her mother says she too knows very little. She apologizes for not speaking English. I always find it strange when people apologize to me for not speaking my native tongue. In America or England, perhaps it would be appropriate. Here in Spain I am the one who should apologize for only speaking English.

Marta's kids are watching a video. There is a little French girl visiting and I am amazed at how Marta switches from speaking French to the children, Flemish to her mother and then back to English with me. She does it effortlessly. I have trouble even expressing myself in English.

She explains the video that the kids are watching. It's a Japanese cartoon called Shin Chan. She likes it because it breaks stereotypes. "Watch" she says and asks her mother which character is the bad guy and which is the good one. Her mother points them out.

Jon, her little boy pipes up; "No, No, Oma, this one is very bad" he points at a tall blond haired blue-eyed hunk, "and this one is the good one" a short, dark, fat ugly man.

Marta's mother shakes her head in disbelief.

"See," Marta says, "it really challenges your stereotypes."

I comment that I've never seen or heard of this cartoon before. Marta says, "It's not shown in other parts of Spain or Europe, only *Catalunya*. They are more open-minded here."

"You mean they want to keep these stereotypes in other parts of Spain?"

"No, it's the main character, the little boy. When he gets angry and upset he shakes his penis or his bottom at people. He knows it's naughty but he does it anyway. In fact, that's why he does it. He knows it upsets the adults. They just can't tolerate that in other parts of Spain. If you and Dennis move away from here, you will run back to *Catalunya* in a year or so. I've seen it before."

The Pharmacy

We are driving to the meditation center in *San Celoni* and I want to stop at a pharmacy to buy some antihistamines. We see an illuminated green cross, the logo of a pharmacy, from the highway and pull into the little town of *Santa Maria de Palautordera*. It's difficult to find parking and the streets are narrow so Dennis drops me off on the corner and I walk up to a pharmacy a few blocks away. There is an old woman waiting outside when I arrive. She starts talking to me immediately and I have to explain "*no entiendo*", I don't understand. It's an early Saturday morning and the shop is supposed to open at 9:00. At 9:15 the doors are still locked. We wait a few minutes more and a car drives up and parks in the no parking zone in front of the shop. A man and a woman dressed in white pharmaceutical coats emerge and they open the shop. Out of nowhere there are suddenly six or seven people waiting in line. I guess the town is small enough that everyone was watching from their windows and doorways for this couple to arrive. They take their place behind glass windows and begin to serve us. I'm third in the queue as we go inside. I ask for antihistamines. She brings out three boxes all different strengths. I'm not sure which one I need. She takes out the information papers from all three boxes and begins to read. A teenager walks in. She's at the back of the queue but is very agitated about a cold sore on her lip and shows it to everybody in line, people are oohing and aahing. The man and woman come out from behind the glass to look at her lip. They discuss with the entire shop which medicine she needs then go back behind the glass. I am still waiting as the woman returns to reading the antihistamine information sheet. I try to tell her I'll take the middle strength ones and point to the package but she just shakes her head and reads. An old man walks in with a branch sticking out of his mouth, literally a branch. Like a giant cigar protruding from his mouth, about 8 inches long and as thick as a broom handle. It has some leaves, still green and fresh sticking out the end. I think he should be at the emergency room at the hospital, not the pharmacy. Once again, the pharmacists come out from behind the counter and have a discussion with the old man and everyone else in the queue. The branch doesn't seem to be the problem, as he mumbles and waves his arms as if it's not there. Twenty minutes later, I walk back to the car to meet Dennis. He said he was getting worried and was going to come and find me. "What could have taken so long?" I guess he didn't see the guy with the branch in his mouth.

Worse than the French

The Spanish bureaucracy can drive even a Spanish bureaucrat *loco*. They have a reputation far worse than Scandinavia and even worse than the French. Because I'm American, I had to apply for a family reunification visa from the Spanish Consulate in Norway before I could legally live here with Dennis. I had to supply our original wedding certificate among a realm of other papers to get the visa. When I finally received my visa the consulate instructed me to show it to the local police as soon as I arrived in Spain. I took my passport to the police station in *Lloret de Mar* and showed them my visa. They told me I was at the wrong police and had to go to the other police. I remembered reading that *Catalunya* has four different police forces; *Policia Nacional, Policia Local, Mossos d'Esquadra* and *Guardia Civil.* Even the locals find difficult it to know which one is responsible for what. At the second police office I showed my visa and was directed to yet another police station. At the third office, the man behind the desk looked at my visa and asked what I wanted. I tried to explain that the embassy told me to show this visa to the police. He asked again, "What do you want?" I was hoping he would tell me so I said "*residencia*". He gave me a slip of paper with an address in *Girona*. Contrary to the embassy's instructions the police weren't interested in seeing my visa at all.

We've decided to wait until after Dennis receives his residence permit before I apply for mine. Then I shouldn't be denied since we will apply for family reunification. A residence card will give me the right to live and work in Spain legally.

Dennis has been notified that his residence paperwork is approved. Driving to *Girona* we can see a thick brown cloud of pollution hanging over the city. The Pyrenees mountains, usually visible in the distance are completely hidden in the haze. It's a Friday and the government offices close early, at 14:00. It's impossible to find parking in the city so we park on the edge of town and walk in. It is a cold 6 Cº in *Girona* this morning. Crossing a bridge into the city, we look down and see thousands of fish waiting in the water far below us. They look like large brown carp with white underbellies. Dennis says he has seen bakeries throw leftover bread into the river at the end of the day so maybe the fish are waiting there to eat.

We are surprised that there's no one waiting at the government office when we walk in. Dennis shows his letter to the man at the desk. He gives us a map to the police station in *Girona* and tells Dennis to show the papers there. We have been there before and found out they do not handle EU citizens so we try to tell him, "*Esta para Noruega*", "It's for Norway", but he refuses to listen.

At the police station, the line is already out the door and around the building. It's still cold out and we are standing in the shade on concrete. After thirty minutes, our feet are freezing and the line has not moved. There is a young couple behind us giving each other big, slurpy, LOUD kisses. I'm tired of listening to them and am starting to get irritated, especially since I don't believe we need to be in this queue. Dennis decides to walk to the security guard at the front desk and show his papers. He comes back about fifteen minutes later and says he was directed to another office where there was no queue and all he needs are some photos so he will go get some made and come back. About thirty minutes later he has handed over his photos and had his fingerprints taken for the *residencia* and they will notify him in six weeks when the card is ready. The *residencia* will be valid for five years so he is very happy.

Dennis has received a letter stating his residence card is ready. It will be a quick trip for him to fetch it so we decide to apply for my residence permit now that his card is ready. We drive to *Girona* and it's warmer and sunnier than the last time we were here. We start at the government office for EU citizens. There is no queue this morning and we move right to the first desk. I take out my passport and try to show the man my visa and ask how to get my *residencia*. He also points to the police station on the map and refuses to look at my passport. We are disappointed, the police station handles everyone outside the European Community and the queues are long and slow.

We wait for about an hour in the queue. The system has changed and this time we are waiting inside the building where it is warmer and quieter. I still feel impatient as the line barely crawls forward. A security guard comes out and says that the office will close at 2:00. It is 12:30 but we take it as a warning that we might not get in. Not sure that we are in the correct queue I decide to show my passport to the security guard at the front desk. He says since I am American, I have to wait here. I tell him "*soy casado con Noruega*", I am married to a Norwegian."

He taps the passport "*Estado Unidos es aqui*", United States is here.

Another guard is listening and argues with first man saying I am married to a Norwegian so I have to go another office. He gives me a map to the office, the very office that refused us three hours ago. I don't want to give up our place in line unless he's sure, so I try to explain that I was there already this morning. I have not learned any past tense in Spanish and know I'm making mistakes. He doesn't understand me so we reluctantly give up our place and head back to the first office.

There are now ten people ahead of us. A man from England just in front of me is complaining loudly about the terrible bureaucracy in Spain. Soon he switches subjects and begins complaining that there are no decent shopping centers in this country. I think he is arrogant to criticize Spain and the very people sitting in this office, assuming no one there understands English. I remember an Intercultural Relations course that I had at my old job. The Swedish man who gave the course had lived in Thailand for many years and was fluent in their language. One day on a flight from Stockholm to Bangkok, he overheard the stewardesses insulting the Swedish passengers in Thai as they were serving drinks. In English they would ask, "Would you like a drink?" then comment in Thai, "you fat ugly slob." Once again in English, "Can I get you anything else?" then in Thai, "you stupid fart." and on and on like that, assuming no one understood a word of Thai. What a shock they got when he thanked them for his drink and the insult in Thai! His first rule of intercultural relations: "don't assume the people around you can't understand your language."

Another forty minutes and we are facing the same man who misdirected us three hours earlier. It's impossible to understand this man; he speaks only Catalan and we don't understand a word. He won't look at my visa, but gives us many papers to fill out and asks if we are married. This looks like the very same paperwork I filled out at the Spanish consulate for my visa. I try to show him my visa but he refuses to look at it. We show him our wedding certificate from Norway, but it is written in Norwegian. He says we have to go to the Norwegian Embassy in Barcelona and get it translated into Spanish. I'm fed up. Our wedding certificate has been approved by the Spanish Embassy; otherwise I would not have a visa. He won't listen to our inadequate attempts at Spanish and won't look at us. We leave frustrated and angry. Outside the office I throw a fit and yell at Dennis. He stays calm and says, "Go ahead and get it out of your system because we are going to have to do exactly what he says. We need to fill out these papers and get our marriage certificate translated and come back and talk to that little Hitler."

Looking for a House

Marta and Carlos knew from the start that we were looking for a house to buy. Carlos told us the first week, "If you want buy a house cheap with some land cheap then you must to go to a place where Jesus left his sandal and not go back and fetch it. This is the way we Spanish say. Do you understand?"

I think about it for a minute, what an interesting expression. "Yes, I understand." I told him, "we say in English *'in the middle of nowhere'*, but I like the Spanish expression better."

We've been pouring over real estate catalogues looking for a house to buy. Every two weeks new catalogues are published and we scan through them looking for any house that sells for 120,000 Euro or less. Of the literally thousands of homes on the market we find three or four per catalogue in our range. Marta tells us that the prices in *Catalunya* have gone up for ten years. "Every year they say, 'This is the top. They can't go higher', but they do." We quickly learn to disregard areas closer to *Barcelona* than *Blanes* or *Hostalrich*.

We visit real estate agents in *Lloret* that advertise some inexpensive homes. The *urbanización* next to the one we live in is what Carlos calls a "working class area" so there might be some cheaper homes there. The agents in *Lloret* refuse to show us the houses. They tell us that we will not like them, or the road is not good, or that we do not want to live there. I've never heard of sales agents discouraging buyers. Marta explains that she experienced this too. She doesn't understand why but one reason might be that people in *Lloret* think that *Lloret* is IT. No one would want to live anywhere else, well maybe *Tossa de Mar*, but certainly not inland. Apart from the fact that I don't like *Lloret*, we simply can't afford it. We soon learn that we have to disregard all the towns directly on the coast all the way to the French border for the prices are at least 20% higher than ten kilometers inland.

A wooden house two streets over is for sale. For some reason people in Spain don't like wooden houses. Marta says that people are afraid of wildfires. She also says it is difficult to get a mortgage for wooden houses. Banks require house insurance and insurance companies don't like to insure wooden houses. They won't come right out and say it though, the bank blames the insurance company and the insurance company blames the bank. Coming from Norway however we love wooden houses. We call the real estate agent and ask about the house but it has been sold.

We look at three more homes with a real estate agent in *Blanes*. The agent is a large, soft-spoken man from Uruguay who speaks a little English. He has lived in Spain for two years and seems to know the market well enough. The first house is in an *urbanización* between *Hostalrich* and *Santa Coloma De Farners*, the county seat. The house is 48 sq. meters (about 500 square feet); brick with a large piece of land but neither the bathroom nor the kitchen are finished. The roads in the *urbanización* are dirt and very eroded but the city has decided to pave them. We find out the cost for the new road will be 9000 Euro per house on top of the sales price, driving the house out of our price range. We have to scratch it off our list. The second house, in the same *urbanización*, is on a beautiful piece of land with stunning views. The home is *prefabricado* a prefabricated modular home, also 48 square meters but we don't look inside. It's simply too much money for what is in essence a mobile home. The third house is in an *urbanización* between *Hostalrich* and *Sils*. It's a long drive from the main road up to the house. The night we visit everyone in the valley is burning leaves and branches and the valley is filled with smoke. The house sits high on a hill and the lot is quite steep. Entering the house, we feel as if we have walked into the third world. This home has been constructed with bits and pieces of scrap metal and wood. I smell mold the instant I walk in and tell the agent we are not interested.

I'm depressed about the prices here. We realized that we have two choices, we move to another part of Spain where prices are cheaper or buy a very small house that probably needs renovation. Having spent the last seven years in Norway fixing an old farmhouse this is a depressing thought.

A few weeks later, I see two houses for sale in *Maçanet de La Selva* in our price range so we make an appointment with an agent in *Vidreres*. The agent is a sophisticated woman with reddish blond hair who speaks a little English. Unlike other agents, she does not try to talk me into a more expensive house instead of the ones I ask to see. Her husband, also a real estate agent, is very friendly and tells me they live in the same *urbanización*, just around the corner from one of the houses we are interested in.

As we drive to look at the two properties, our expectations are low. The properties are about four kilometers from the pueblo of *Maçanet de La Selva*. A wild fire swept through the area last summer and we see burned trees everywhere. The lush undergrowth is completely burned away and the land looks scarred and sad. The agent points to a burned hillside and tells us there used to be eucalyptus trees there. She said the community acted too slowly and the fire got way out of control. She warns us the houses we will look at have some trees damaged. "No one lost a house, but the fire went everywhere." The first property actually has two houses on a nice piece of land. The main house is wooden and faces the A7 highway but is far enough away that there is not much highway noise. There is an illegally built grandmother house behind the main house. The agent assures us this is no problem. The house has been there more than 5 years so the government can't make you remove it. There is also a beautiful barbecue area with covered arches and a large built in stone table. The biggest problem we see is that the main house has no insulation and there is no heating. One wall in the bathroom is rotten and we can see daylight through some cracks in the room joints. This is definitely a summer home, not a year round residence.

The second property is of traditional construction, brick with stucco. It's 50 square meters and sits low on a hillside with a plot of land reaching down the hill to a small stream in the gully below. We see that the wild fire swept through the valley surrounding the house. The trees are completely charred and the normally lush foliage underneath is gone. The cork oak survived and is starting to send out new shoots. The agent tells me, "they are strong trees, the cork oak" as she makes a fist with both hands. I think the fire must have been terrifying sweeping so near the houses and it is amazing nothing but landscaping was burned. There's a stately palm tree at the driveway entrance with a charred trunk. There must have been trees lining the fence surrounding the property for the fence is black with soot and there are burned stumps in the ground. The house is nearly new and we like it immediately. The bathroom is as tiny as can be, just large enough to hold a shower, a toilet and a sink. There isn't even a towel rack. One bedroom; although called *doble* (double) is tiny and will never hold our bed bought in Norway. The second bedroom is almost as small as the bathroom. There are no closets, but nonetheless we like the house very much. The kitchen is new with an oven, gas stove and refrigerator. The floors are tiled with a peach ceramic tile and the walls are white washed. Even though it's small, it feels light and airy. We could possibly enclose a large porch for a separate dining room.

Marta calls later that day. She is going to drive to Andorra tomorrow with the kids to visit Carlos. He has rented a small cottage for a week and paid for skiing lessons for the children. She called to ask us about driving in the snow. Does she need chains? We recommend them of course. After years in Norway, we don't hesitate, "You need proper equipment to drive on snow and ice." We tell her about the house that we've just looked at. She wants to see it immediately but there is no time before her trip. We promise to show her when she gets back. She recommends, "If you really do like the house—act fast. Don't let it get away."

We debate whether to buy a house right now or not. We've only lived here four months. Is it long enough to make a commitment? Is this the right time to buy? Maybe the prices will start falling and we should wait? The exchange rate from Norwegian *kroner* to euro has never been worse. If we wait, will it improve? Marta says she can rent her house in the summer so we can get out of our contract early. We would save some money not paying rent and not paying to store our furniture in Norway. What should we do?

We like the house but we don't love it. It doesn't pull at our heartstrings. Our house in Norway was a love affair; a large wooden, hundred year old, two story farmhouse in the country. It was a dream come true. Maybe I don't want another house that I love. It hurt so much to sell it.

We consider the location of the little house. It's an hour by train to *Barcelona*, about twenty minutes from *Girona*, its thirty minutes from the beach, thirty minutes from the mountains and five minutes from the small town of *Maçanet* which has shops, restaurants, a post office and even a veterinarian. It's ten kilometers from *Vidreres*, which is a small town we like, and fifteen minutes from *Blanes*, a large city with another train line to *Barcelona*. It is one of the smallest and least expensive houses in a good area. We will look at the little house one more time and if we both still like it we will make an offer. We start transferring money from Norway to put a security deposit on the house, just in case we decide to buy it.

I'm nervous when we meet the agent at the house and we examine it more carefully. We notice that there are some cracked tiles in the living room and bathroom and the walls are painted concrete-not plastered. The butane tank for the stove and hot water is inside one of the kitchen cabinets. We would prefer it to be outside. The agent tells us this is normal. Dennis would need to put up a fence around the property to keep our cats in and the neighborhood dogs out. There is a cistern on the property and gutters to collect water from the roof. We like the house and property very much and decide to make an offer. After some negotiation we agree on a price-our maximum exactly matches the owner's minimum. The agent takes out a sample of the sales agreement and tries to explain it to us. She starts having trouble with her English. We ask if there is any debt on the property and she thinks we are asking if someone is DEAD on the property. "No," she tells us, "there are no ghosts here." We have to write the word *debt* on a piece of paper before she understands. We take a copy home to study. We agree to meet at her office in three days to sign the agreement and pay a 10% deposit.

She tells us the husband in the family is very ill. If he cannot come, the daughter will sign in his place. We are shaky as we drive home. We are buying a house in Spain!

No Pay, No Water

Two young men are wandering in front of our rental house and shaking the gate. I walk out to see what they want. They start to speak in Spanish and I interrupt them, "*No hablo muy español.*"

One asks, "English?" and I answer, "*Si.*" It's always difficult for me to switch back and forth between languages.

He squeezes his eyebrows, searching for words, then tells me simply, "no pay, no water."

We've been renting for four months and have not seen a water bill. We did not know how often they billed and assumed Marta would let us know. I tell them, "*alquilamos,*" we rent.

One of them shakes his head in sympathy. "Talk to proprietor," he says and repeats, "no pay, no water."

I ask, "*Cuando?*" When?

He says, "*por la tarde.*"

I am shocked, this means in a couple of hours we will have no water, won't even be able to flush the toilet.

I ask; "TODAY?"

He nods, "Yes today." He gives me a business card for the water company and tells me to call the office.

Marta is in Andorra so I can't reach her. I call the water office but no one can speak English and they can't understand me. We decide to drive to the office in *Llagostera*, about forty minutes up the coast and try to pay the bill. We stop in town and ask at a bakery where the water company is. We are pointed to the city square. We don't see it and ask a man on the street. He gives us complicated directions three rights and down a hill and left but there is no parking. We try to find it and don't see the street. We have to ask again. Once again, we are directed one street up, turn right and then left. We still can't find it and the street names are not correct. We look for the *ayuntamiento,* the town hall, where they often have good information and maps, but cannot find it. We stop again and two old men who tell us to drive out of town, to *industrial.* This sounds promising so we head east from town. There's a young man laying brick on the sidewalk. I show him the business card of the water company and he gives us instructions that are more detailed. I don't understand his words but remember his hand movements. Finally, we see the street name and know we are close. One more stop, one more question and we find the office.

We give them our address and Dennis quotes the young man at our gate, "*no pagar, no aqua.*" The woman searches through a file cabinet then brings us a bill. We both go into shock. It's 638.00 Euros. There is no address on the bill, only a *parcela* number, a lot number. The name on the account is not Marta's. Dennis wants to go to the bank and pay it. He tells me, "Marta never notified the water company when she bought the house." We argue in the office. I don't want to pay it. It's so much money and we don't even know if it's the right bill. We leave deciding to live without water for a few days until Marta returns from Andorra. When we get home we fill old water jugs with tap water preparing for a dry week-end.

Later, Marta explains that she tried to change the name and address on the water bill last summer but she never heard anything from the water company. Completely adapted to the Spanish way of life she then promptly forgot about the problem.

Teaching English

Marta called this evening and asks if I want to teach English. I was planning to look for a job as soon as we have settled into a new house. She teaches English, German, French and Spanish for various language academies. Her language academy in *Calella* just lost a teacher who had worked there for twelve years. They desperately need someone to teach classes starting next week. I say yes immediately. It's not often a job comes knocking at the door.

I am supposed to have four students but only two come regularly. Both are men in their twenties. They are rank beginners in English, my favorite level. I love the fast learning curve of beginners. You can almost see them absorbing the language. These two young men are no exception, and with only two students they learn English much faster than I am learning Spanish in a class of thirty.

On the first day of class, after introductions, I play a game to warm up. I write these two sentences on the board:

I love _____, _____, _____
I hate _____, _____, _____.

I draw a big heart around the word **love** and a frowning face around the word **hate**, so they understand the meanings. In the blanks I draw pictures of three things I love: cats, gardening, meditation and make them guess the words. Of course they guess in Spanish but I then teach them the English word. We continue with three things I hate: TV, coconut, war. My pictures are not very good and it takes a while for them to guess, but its fun. Now it's their turn to draw. I give them a few minutes to draw on paper first and then make them go to the board. I discover that my two students have nearly opposite personalities. One loves: big cities, motorcycles, and discos. The other loves: dogs, TV and walking in the country. One hates religion, soup and rules. The other hates cats, motorcycles and apples. I love this game because we get to know each other a little and they learn so much the first day; two verbs **love** and **hate**; the personal pronoun **I** and twenty four new words.

It's challenging for me to teach when I can't speak Spanish. It's easy enough with nouns, like **book** and **chair**, but how do you explain the difference between the words **what** and **which**? How do you explain what **very** means, or **quite**? I know I should be able to teach without using the student's mother tongue. I learned Norwegian from teachers who never spoke English. During my TEFL[1] certification, we were taught Russian using no English, just to demonstrate that it is possible. If my students came from different countries, then I would make the effort to avoid Spanish; but I do resort to looking words up in the Spanish dictionary. I use the excuse that it will help me learn Spanish.

My classes are from 8:00 to 10:00 in the evenings. I am amazed that my students are able to learn at this time of night after a long day of work. This is another example of how different the Spanish are. They are used to late, late hours. Many don't even eat dinner until 11:00 at night and stay up long past midnight on weekdays. They simply don't sleep much.

I drill and drill the students on pronunciation. I want them to drop their heavy accents; change *"theeze"* to **"this"** and *"shanuary"* to **"January."** They can repeat perfectly when I drill them, but when they read aloud, they fall back into their old habits. One of them tries to help me with my Spanish. He tells me to put a pencil in my mouth when I talk and I will get the right sound. I try it and it really works, but kind of makes my mouth sore.

I enjoy teaching, but it is challenging. I make mistakes that create difficulties for my students. Sometimes I use examples with more complicated grammar than they have had up to date, and have to scratch it out and apologize. I have to constantly remind myself to simplify, simplify, simplify.

---

1.   Teaching English as a Foreign Language

Barcelona

Occasionally we take the train to *Barcelona* and spend the entire day. With more than two million people in the city and another two million in the surrounding districts, it's an enormous place. It enchants me. It is big, noisy and polluted but it enchants me. We exit the train at *Plaça de Catalunya*. The plaza is filled with people when we arrive at 10:00 in the morning. Day or night, the city is always full of people. Sidewalk cafes and shopping centers surround the square. We are inundated by traffic noise and exhaust fumes. We walk north up *Passeig de Gracia* and look at an apartment designed by Antoni Gaudi, called *Casa Battló*. It was been closed to the public for many years. In the year 2000, to celebrate 150 years since Gaudi's birth, it was opened to the public. It's an amazing building. With no square edges, no straight lines it feels organic, alive. Dennis does not want to pay the 16.00 Euro fee to enter so I try to describe the interior to him as we stand outside. I find my words are inadequate and give up. He simply must see it for himself.

Walking north and east there are designer shops with highly polished boots in the windows, gowns with plunging necklines, with embedded pearls and giant bows for the rich and famous, bakeries with stacks of crunchy fried *churros* and homemade biscotti. There's an entire shop filled with chocolates so exclusive that they are priced by individual pieces. At the next Gaudi building *Casa Pedrera* there is a long line of people waiting to get in. We join the queue and while we wait people stop and ask us questions in Spanish, French and German. Each time we have to shake our heads no, "only English." *Casa Pedrera* is wonderful, especially the surrealistic, mosaic covered chimneys on the rooftop. The crowds make it difficult to enjoy though and soon we are longing for a place to sit in peace and quiet.

We walk west on avenue *Provence* and stop for a *café solo*, the Spanish espresso, at a sidewalk café. Peace and quiet is elusive in Spain but we do find wonderful pastries and can't resist. Dennis orders a chocolate filled pastry shaped like a large piece of cannelloni. I order a *xhou xhou* (in Catalan pronounced choo, choo like a train) a cream filled, croissant shaped donut sprinkled with sugar. The café is full of cigarette smoke so we don't linger. A short time later, we continue our walk.

Suddenly we are stunned at the sight of Gaudi's most famous building the *Sagrada Familia*. We have seen it before but each time the reality of it staggers the imagination. I read that Gaudi's teachers couldn't decide if he was crazy or was a genius. When I see this church, I am convinced he was both. Its narrow stone towers shoot into the air, like rockets out of the Stone Age. We try to ascend one of the towers but the narrow winding staircase and thick, stone walls give me claustrophobia. Biting back the urge to scream, I turn around and head back down the tiny stairway. There is a tourist on every step and I force them all to scrunch to the side as I descend. I feel like kissing the ground as I reach the last turn and breathe deeply. I've just read Washington Irving's <u>Tales of Alhambra</u> and think of the poor souls imprisoned in dungeons with these kind of thick walls and tiny windows. I would have lasted about an hour, before going stark raving mad. I walk to the interior of the church. Part of the interior is filled with stone columns that branch at the top, like giant oaks, supporting the roof. I look up at the towers soaring hundreds of meters into the air. I imagine Dennis ascending around and around inside one of them. Clouds are passing overhead and it gives the illusion of the towers swaying, making me dizzy. I exit through the western nave and wait in the sunshine for Dennis.

Finding an empty spot, I join a crowd of people sitting on a wide concrete banister of a stairway that leads down to a park below the church. There are teams of people milling around a square in the middle of the park. Someone is yelling through a loud speaker. Soon a group of men, women and children, all dressed in white pants, green shirts and wide black belts begin to climb on top of each other. What luck! This is my first chance to see the famous *Castellers*, the human towers, of *Catalunya*. First one layer of sturdy men makes a circle inter-linking arms. Then a second layer stands on the shoulders of the first and a third layer on their shoulders. I'm close enough to see the people on the bottom trembling from the weight and swaying. A fourth layer is added then finally, a child climbs up the backs and shoulders of the others. She grabs anything to keep steady, clothes, arms and hair in her climb, until she finally squats on someone's shoulders at the very top and waves one hand in the air. I'm surprised that women as well as men are forming the towers. There seems to be a competition with a new tower forming every fifteen minutes or so. The crowd cheers each team on. One little girl loses her balance just as she reaches the top. She falls, dragging the tower down on top of her. Caught by people in the crowd, she is unhurt but frightened and starts crying. She's handed over to her teammates as they stand and brush themselves off.

Any street we walk in Barcelona is entertaining. We pass a beautiful building. The lower floors are renaissance style but they are topped with large black towers trimmed in gold in the style of Russian mosques. A flock of bright green parrots swarm down on us from the rooftops and disappear into the tree-lined street. A street vendor sells barbecued sweet potatoes off a smoldering grill on a street corner. There's a marquee showing two naked men and advertising a comedy show 'Penis puppets'. We see a beggar sitting wrapped in a blanket with two dogs sleeping on the sidewalk at his feet. On the end of tiny, tiny chains are three meager kittens crawling over his body.

Another day, another visit we head down *Passeig de Sant Joan* to the *Arc de Triumpf.* The city market at *Arc de Triumf* is closed for the afternoon so we continue south to *Parc de la Ciutadella.* People are strolling slowly through the grass and trees, walking dogs, biking or sleeping off their lunches. A bride and groom are having their pictures taken at the small lake in the city park. We admire the beauty of *La Cascada,* a thundering waterfall with a combination of ragged rocks and classical sculptures. Turning west, we walk back along the waterfront toward *La Rambla.* We see a massive sculpture that looks like a giant paperclip standing on end, but slightly bent out of shape. Another sculpture looks like a gigantic wire meshed lobster trap suspended in the air above the buildings.

Taking a small detour at *Port Vell* we see sidewalk vendors laying out sheets on the ground and displaying CDs and videos for sale, all copies, all probably illegal. The movable bridge is lined with people, reading, kissing and sitting in the fading sun. There are two street musicians trying to play country western music and failing miserably.

We visit the city market, the famous *Boqueria* where it's impossible to capture in words the variety of fruits and vegetables, the colors and the SMELLS. I fall in love with a small sculpture of a pig with a huge belly sitting on a meat counter. While browsing in a small wine stall, we see an old hunchback gypsy woman carrying a brown bag with a horse's hoof, fur and all, sticking out of the top. Is she going to make soup?

At *La Rambla, Barcelona*'s most famous promenade, we see a man dressed in an elf costume trying to crawl inside a giant cardboard mushroom. There's another man dressed as an angel gilded from head to toe and glowing in the afternoon sun. Every restaurant has identical menus, identical billboards; sun bleached pictures of different kinds of *paella* for sale. There's a street artist balancing on a bike. He's perfectly still but somehow he has wired his clothing so it looks like he's riding extremely fast. His jacket is swept in the air behind his back and his tie also swept behind his neck. Another street artist is completely painted silver and dressed like Little Bow Peep with silver ceramic sheep. There are artists selling paintings and offering to do mediocre portraits. Street vendors are selling everything from newspapers and magazines to chicks and rabbits in cages. There are flowers for sale, their bright colors lining the stalls. Sidewalk cafés advertise *churros con chocolate*. A group of men and women are playing the cup game, trying to lure people to gamble. We've been warned away from these. Not only is it a con game but a locale for pickpockets. There's a puppeteer, with a meter high puppet dressed in a black tuxedo playing a toy piano. The puppet draws a big crowd. Beethoven's 5th symphony is blaring from a loudspeaker and the puppet's actions are perfectly synchronized to the music. All the while, we are strongly aware of possible pickpockets, especially here, especially on *La Rambla*.

We walk back through the gothic quarter, the original city of Barcelona, with the narrow cobblestone streets and dark alleyways. Clothing shops, restaurants and bars line the streets. There are all kinds of specialty shops selling hats, shoes, and pajamas. There's one shop that sells nothing but beads, another with only racks; coat racks, tie racks, kitchen racks, etc. One shop has one hundred kinds of green tea and is decorated like an apartment from the 1960's with orange furniture, green carpet and black lights on the wall. There are churches everywhere with the main Cathedral sitting boldly in the city square. I'm shocked to see some of the smaller churches painted with graffiti. The smells in this old quarter of the city are overwhelming; mold and dog shit mixed with cigarette smoke, coffee, warm pizza and grilled chicken. I lived in an apartment on one of these narrow streets during my teacher training. As we walk by I feel a mixture of nostalgia and revulsion. With streets only as wide as a car with tall buildings on either side, there's little sunlight or fresh air. They are so narrow and dark that when we take a picture from the middle of the street on a bright sunny day the flash goes off.

Living in Limbo

Sometimes I feel as if I am in limbo living here in Spain. Like one of those spider webs that detaches and floats away in the breeze. I am waiting to land, to find a point of connection. When we moved to Norway, it was on a contract with a company I had been with for years. The work routines were familiar. I walked the same route to work everyday, saw the same people for eight hours everyday. Somehow that gave me a sense of belonging. I have no sense of belonging here. In our Spanish classes the students' cluster with others from the same country, the same language. There's a group of French women, a group of Russian men, a group of African men, a couple from Italy, two women from England, two women from India and Dennis and I. We greet each other with *hola* and *buenas* but other than that, there is little interaction. Even when we try, we don't have enough language in common to interact more.

A film clip of Basque terrorists was on TV last night. They wore black stocking masks and carried guns. The only word I understood in the newscast was *Catalunya*. Were they declaring a new terror campaign? On TV, we watch the Spanish president Jose Maria Aznar commenting on the Basque declaration, obviously unhappy. I have no idea what he is saying. Are we going to have bomb threats here in *Lloret de Mar*? I go to the Norwegian Internet page for the Oslo newspaper *Aftenposten* to find out what has happened. Relieved I learn that the terrorists have declared a cease-fire for *Catalunya*. The Spanish government is upset. They think the Catalan Nationalists have negotiated a special agreement with the Basque Nationalists. The terrorists said this agreement was to 'unite oppressed peoples.' Spain's central government wants a total arms rest for all of Spain, not an autonomous region negotiating on its own. There is a national election coming in March and this might influence the outcome. Fervor for independence is rampant in different regions of Spain. Here in *Catalunya*, the people call themselves, not a state, but *un pais,* a country. How are they oppressed by the Spanish state? The *Generalitat de Catalunya*, the regional government has wide powers over education, health, trade, industry, tourism and agriculture. We feel ourselves outsiders. We don't understand this conflict.

I hate the simple question, "Where are you from?" I haven't lived in the United States for ten years and don't feel I give a correct picture by just saying I'm American. Frankly, I am embarrassed to say I am American. I'm embarrassed by the atrocities of my government toward other cultures, toward the environment, abuses of the Geneva Convention and human rights. Since the bombing of the world trade centers in New York, the USA government has decreed the right to preemptive strike. The concept is appalling to me. Could any other nation justify an agenda that says: attack first just to be sure? Didn't Hitler use that as an excuse to rampage Europe? Watching American news or interviews on TV, the country feels more foreign to me than Norway. Yet, I can't really say I'm from Norway. At one time, I felt it was home but now that we are living in Spain that connection is fading. We've lived in America, Australia, Norway and now, Spain. Where am I from? Every country has left an imprint, indelible marks on my beliefs, customs, on my way of life. My ideal country would be a combination of them all.

Another difficult question is, "Why are you in Spain?" It's not easy to answer. We lost our jobs in Norway. We wanted to retire early and needed a cheap place to live. We were tired of the long winters and extreme cold. We want to learn Spanish. The taxes and cost of living are too high in Norway. The long hours of darkness were too depressing in the winter. We like the openness of the people in Spain. Spain is an interesting country culturally and geographically. The food is very good and very cheap here. I missed people who chat with strangers. More sun. *Barcelona*. National health care.

I've read that it's emotionally more confusing to be an expatriate than to be an immigrant. The very fact that you have a choice in the matter creates ambivalences in which refugees or immigrants don't have the luxury of indulging. Maybe that is the reason for this limbo. I don't have a home. More to the point, I can't really figure out where home is. And so I wonder when we will land. I wonder IF we will land.

Breakfast Sausages and a Morning Walk

Marta invites us for breakfast and a walk on a rainy Tuesday morning in February. Her kids are in school and her classes in *Barcelona* were cancelled so she has the morning free. She wants us to try a Catalan specialty *botifarra*. There's a small restaurant in *Vidreres* that grills these spicy pork sausages *a la brasa*, over an open fireplace. The sausages are served with *pa amb tomāquet*, grilled bread served with raw garlic and fresh tomato. The air is cold outside and as we enter the restaurant, the fireplace warms us immediately. We've hit the breakfast rush hour and the restaurant is full; old men sitting by themselves at the bar, groups of men young and old at the tables. There's a man with white hair and a large belly sitting on a small stool in front of the fireplace. His shirt is open at the top and I can see white chest hairs sticking out. On the table next to him are platters of raw sausage and slices of bread. He's leaning over the fire carefully grilling sausage and bread on a rack. Is this the chef?

We order *botifarras* and the waitress brings a basket of fresh tomatoes, garlic cloves and a bottle of olive oil to the table. Marta says normally *botifarra* is ordered with red wine but at 10:00 in the morning, we all opt for strong black coffee. I watch an old man walk slowly to the bar. He's tall and gaunt; his hair is so white it glows. He's wearing it long, to his shoulders but it's so thin I can see his pink scalp shining underneath. He's frail but dignified. As he sits down the bartender greets him with *bon dia* then places a tall fluted glass and a bottle of *cava*, the Spanish champagne, in front of him. There was no conversation so I assume that this is his usual order. He opens the bottle and pours a glass and with a shaky hand takes a sip. A big smile comes across his face, now he is content. Our sausages arrive and they have a wonderful smoky charred taste. The combination of sausage and bread is perfect. This is finger food and our hands come away smelling of garlic and olive oil. My sausage is too big to finish and Dennis eats the last few bites. I walk over to the waitress to order more coffee. As I open my mouth to speak, I can smell garlic on my own breath.

Marta tells us about her trip to Andorra and her kid's first time on skis. Her seven-year-old daughter was a natural fearless skier and picked it up the first day. Her nine-year-old son, the more cautious type, took the whole week to get comfortable but finally managed a downhill run on the last day. She is amazed at how different her children are, one confident and fearless, the other careful and cautious.

Carlos is doing well and was very excited to see them. She asked him if he was coming back to work in *Lloret* when the season was over in Andorra and he was non-committal, so she didn't press him. "I can't hold on to someone if they don't want to be held," she tells us. Marta said she finally figured out why his drinking bothered her so much and told Carlos. It hurts her that he prefers to drink alone in a bar rather than be at home with her and the kids. Carlos took all the blame, saying, "I'm not a nice person."

A few days later, however, Carlos called and asked Marta to send him addresses of some hotels in *Lloret*. She didn't understand why he needed them and thought it was for some clients in Andorra so she told him she was too busy. In a hurt voice he told her, "I can always work in Canaries." Marta suddenly realized he was telling her he wanted to come home. She was so happy. "I told him 'Yes, yes, I'll even send them DHL if you want'. He liked that," she beams; "I'm so happy he's coming back."

After breakfast, we walk to the end of town then head west toward farmland. We walk on a dirt road weaving and dodging puddles and mud. The land is beautiful and we see wild blackberry vines lining both sides of the dirt road. We pass *fincas* or farmhouses, big stone buildings in various states of disrepair. Marta explains that when she first came to Spain in the early 1990's she almost bought a *finca*. "They were reasonable back then." Then she decided being a single woman, she would feel better having neighbors. "Today, you can't touch one," she tells us, "their prices are so high."

The road merges into an *urbanización* as the clouds start to clear and we can barely see the huge outline of *Mt. Montseny* on the horizon. The weather stays cold though and our noses are runny. Dennis takes off his raincoat and slings it over his shoulder. Marta and I stay bundled up. At every house, from behind fences, dogs bark and jump at us as we walk through the subdivision. Today we are noticing fences and commenting on different designs, the thoughts of the house we are going to buy in the front of our minds.

No Speed Limits, Park Anywhere

We're terrified of the way people drive here. In all fairness, tourists probably do a lot of the bad driving but it really is incredible what drivers will do. The moped drivers are the worst, buzzing around ignoring lanes, lights, and stop signs. Driving near the university in *Barcelona* is harrowing, where there can be dozens of mopeds weaving around your car at the same time. Their equivalent in *Blanes* and *Lloret* are the *telepizza* mopeds. I have seen them cut off semi-trucks, drive the wrong way around a roundabout, drive on the wrong side of construction barriers, run red lights and drive down the center line on a major highway with high speed traffic in both directions.

Spanish drivers completely ignore two signs: speed limits and no parking. Driving 20 kph over the speed limit is expected, 30-40 kph is normal with a few crazies who drive as fast as possible and as often as possible, regardless of school zones, cross walks and shopping districts. People do park anywhere and everywhere; on sidewalks, blocking intersections, in bus stops, under no parking signs, on train tracks. We've been double parked so many times we can't count. Most of the times there have been plenty of free parking spaces so they could have parked elsewhere but chose not to. How can they be so thoughtless?

One day I had to make a left turn on a two-lane highway. This meant stopping traffic in my lane until the oncoming traffic was clear. Most of the people behind me tried to drive on the right shoulder to pass me, which is to be expected. Some crazy persons actually tried to pass me on the left. This meant that, not only did I have to watch for oncoming traffic but, I also had to watch for traffic coming up from behind me.

Trying to get to Spanish class one morning, we are stuck at a busy intersection near the weekly market in *Lloret*. One man actually gets out of his truck and goes into a nearby shop, blocking the only lane of traffic. We and fifty other cars sit through three traffic lights until the driver finally returns with coffee and donuts and gets back into his truck.

One day we see the police loading body bags into a van on the side of the highway *Nacional*. I'm completely unsettled by the sight. A few hours ago we had seen two prostitutes standing on the road at this very spot. I don't know if they are the ones who died or if it was motorists. Life suddenly seems so fragile. I want to grab Dennis's hand and hold on.

Bombings in Madrid

It's the middle of March and Dennis turns on the TV at lunchtime. Every channel has pictures of the *Atoche* train station in *Madrid*. At first we think there has been a crash but soon we realize it was bombed. Everyone suspects ETA, the Basque terrorist group who has been in the news so much lately. We can't believe the pictures of the bombings, there are bodies lying on the ground, ignored by rescue workers as they rush to help the living. One of the rescue workers is interviewed. We can't understand what he is saying but he breaks down and cries halfway through the interview. I feel like I am re-living Sept 11th. I get on the Internet and look at the Norwegian newspaper *Aftenposten* to find out what has happened. Thirteen bombs have exploded at three different train stations in *Madrid*. Over 150 people are dead and counting. No one has claimed responsibility yet.

Spain is grieving. Every shop window, doorway, every TV station and school desk displays a looped black ribbon, a sign of mourning. There is a fifteen-minute period of silence planned for noon today, in memory of the victims. We are in *Blanes* when all the shops close down and people stand on the street in silence, staring into space.

People have posted signs everywhere declaring, "No to Terrorism" and "We Support the Victims and Their Families." ETA has denied responsibility although the government is claiming they are responsible. Others are saying it might have been the terrorist group al Qaeda.

Families of the victims are interviewed on television every day. The victims were working class people living in apartments outside of *Madrid*. They walked their children to school in the mornings then caught the train into the city to go to work. They worked in restaurants, kiosks and department stores. They were people like you and I. One first grade classroom lost six parents. One child lost her mother, father and grandfather in the same day; all were riding the same train.

We read about one family in the English section of the Spanish newspaper *El Pais* and I can't get the story out of my mind. A young man was wounded. The authorities found his name but no other identification. A family from *Murcia* contacted the authorities. Their son of the same name was missing; believed to be on the train that fateful morning in Madrid. The family traveled from *Murcia* to *Madrid* to visit the young man in the hospital. He was the right size and build but was so bruised and beaten that they hardly recognized him. Later a young woman contacted the authorities. She was missing her fiancé; he too had the same name. She visited the young man in the hospital. "It's my fiancé," she declares. Both families desperate to know—which person was he? It wasn't until days later when the man finally regained consciousness that the young woman could rejoice and the family from *Murcia* go home to grieve. Their son had been killed.

America seemed to change after the attacks of 9/11. People seem more afraid than ever. The government has declared a strange kind of war giving them the right to incarcerate people at the drop of a hat. Those who dare to speak against the government are beaten up, loose their jobs and are called unpatriotic. I don't want this to happen to Spain. This is a lovely country where the people are friendly and open, welcoming of strangers. Spaniards are masters of the art of relaxation and enjoying life. I don't want to see it replaced by fear and anger.

I have hope for Spain. TV stations are flooded with pictures of mass demonstrations; spontaneous gatherings in the streets of all the major cities. Over eleven million people turn out to honor the families of the dead, protest terrorism, and grieve for the lost.

Consumed by the horror of the bombings we try to follow the news. The PP[1] controlled government is still blaming ETA for the bombings although the evidence is now pointing to a group loosely connected to al Qaeda. Spain's involvement in the war in Iraq is wildly unpopular and the current government does not want the Madrid bombings connected to that war in any way. Nonetheless, all the evidence points in that direction. Three days after the bombings there are national elections and a new government has been voted in. People are angry that the old government involved Spain in the war on Iraq. They are angry that it misled them about the bombings. The new government promises to withdraw troops from Iraq. International commentators say Spain has given in to terrorists by turning on its own government. I ask my Spanish students how they feel about the change of government. They can't express themselves well in English but both think it is good. One manages to tell me that any government is better than the old one.

---

1.   Partido Popular

Carlos comes home from Andorra and I ask him how he feels about the change of government. He's also thinks it's good. He explains; "The new government will talk to people instead of charging like a bull. Ninety percent of Spain not wanted war to Iraq. Every party in government say no except the PP. Parliament even asked for a national referendum to decide if we go to war, but the government refuse." Carlos shakes his head in disgust. "I like Zapatero.[2] England and America say we are afraid, we're not. Well we are, but that not the reason we change governments. What have we to do making war on that country Iraq? You remember those pictures from *Azores* with Bush and Tony Blair and Aznar[3]? All those newspaper taking photos? Aznar was puffed up like a bird, saying 'look at me with the big countries'. Well, Zapatero says he is removing Spain from that picture. We Spanish, we like that, we not want Spain in that picture."

---

2. The newly elected president: José Luis Rodríguez Zapatero.
3. José Maria Aznar, the previous president, invited President Bush and Prime Minister Blair to the Azores where they announced that Spain would be sending troops to Iraq with the USA and Britain.

You Have to Get Your Own Saint

We meet the owners of the house we will buy at our real estate agent's office. It's a tiny office and there are nine of us crammed in front of her desk. The agent's husband, daughter and son-in-law are there as well as the husband, wife and daughter who own the property. Our agent has explained that the husband in the family is very ill. The family had planned to retire in this house but now it's impossible. We can see that he is very sick as soon as we meet him. He is thin, almost emaciated and walks with effort. His wife has that typical look of a middle aged Spanish woman, short and very round. The daughter is chain smoking, filling the small room with smoke. I wonder if she is nervous. As we read the paperwork and prepare to hand over the 10% deposit the wife breaks out in a long dialog waving her arms at our real estate agent. Finally, she breaks down and cries. I'm sitting next to her and instinctively put my hand on her shoulder to comfort her. I feel guilty for wanting to buy the house although I know they need to sell it. Dennis points at me and tells everyone in the office, "She cried for a month when we sold our house in Norway!"

Our agent says, "Really!" and translates this for everyone in the room. They all turn and stare at me.

The woman asks me; "*Es verdad?*" "Is it true?"

I nod, "Yes. It broke my heart to sell our house there." She grabs my hand and starts rattling off in Catalan. I don't understand a word but the ice is broken. Suddenly we all feel a little better.

Our real estate agent explains that the owners need our 10 percent payment to pay off the architect and the fee for the house permit. Before the house can be sold we have to wait two or three weeks for the paperwork to be finished at the government office. Then we will meet at the *notario's* office to make the final payment.

The owners want us to meet them at the house so they can show us around. We drive in separate cars to the house. We have to follow them to the house because the streets in the *urbanización* are like a maze. I count them while Dennis drives; left, two streets, right, left, right, two streets right, left, left, right and we are finally there. They unlock the gate and the woman walks me to the front door as Dennis follows the husband to the cistern near the road. We enter the house and it's cool and dark. The woman opens the shutters then walks around touching everything in the house lovingly. She repeatedly grabs her heart and explains that she is leaving all the furniture, dishes, silverware, garden tools, TV, washing machine, refrigerator; in essence everything needed to live there. I am shocked at their generosity. And repeat "*es verdad?*" Is it true? The man is weak but tries to take Dennis around and show him the water and septic systems. The daughter shows me the fruit trees in the garden, nothing is in bloom yet and I'm not sure what they are. The only word I understand is *higo*, fig. Everything examined, the woman goes back inside the house and grabs a ceramic Saint off the bedroom wall. She kisses it as she tucks it under her arm. She tells me: you have to get our own Saint. She also grabs a coffee machine as she walks out the door saying it's for her daughter and the tour is over. They get in the car and leave. I tell Dennis about their generosity and show him all the dishes and pots and pans that they are leaving. We even find two *paella* pans hanging in the laundry room outside. He finds heavy iron garden tools and some spare tiles and paint. We are in shock and don't feel like we should touch anything. It's not ours yet.

We're nervous buying this house. One of the books we've read[1] recommends a series of steps to ensure you aren't screwed. We read the list and write it down point by point. I try to go through the list with our agent but she simply answers, "Of course, of course," to every question. We press our agent on what we think are the most important things. Is there any debt on the property? Is the title clear? She assures us that there are no problems. We want to trust her, and in reality have to trust her because we cannot read well enough to do this without her. I like the fact that our agent lives a couple of blocks from our house in the same *urbanización*. If we are screwed, it will be right in her face, so to speak.

The date is set for the final payment and the closing at a *notario* in the town of *Santa Coloma de Farners*. In three weeks, we will be the proud owners of a tiny house in Spain. We're nervous as hell.

---

1.   Harry King (2002, *Buying a Property in Spain*, How to Books Ltd., UK

Home but No Phone

We order a check from our Spanish bank a few days before the closing. They say it will take a few days so we are glad we started early. The check is not ready until the morning of the closing making us even more nervous. We pick up the check and drive to *Santa Coloma*. I notice in the bankbook that they have charged a whopping 800 Euro for issuing the check. That's almost a one-month budget for us. I can't believe it and want to go back and complain, but it's too late; we are due at the *notario's* office soon. I've always thought our Spanish bank had high fees but this is ridiculous. It feels like extortion.

We meet the real estate agent and the owners of the house at the *notario's* office in *Santa Coloma de Farners*. Everything goes smoothly. The papers are signed and the money is paid. We are given a "*copia simple*", a copy of the official document called "*escritur publica*" that will be sent to us in a few months with the signatures and stamps from the property register. We are given the keys and we shake hands with the old owners and depart in a daze. We drive out to visit our new house and I feel like a voyeur, snooping into another person's life. The old owners left nearly everything. There are clothes in the closet and liquor in the cupboards. There's even a bottle of champagne. Our household goods should be arriving from Norway in a couple of weeks. After six months of living out of two suitcases, we are trying to remember what we have stored away. Where are we going to put everything in this tiny house?

Dennis is installing a fence around the house. We want to keep the neighborhood dogs out and our cats in. I go with him to the house and spend a few hours working in the garden. The neighbors stop by and say *bon dia*. Most of them are just weekend residents, escaping small apartments in the city for the weekend. A few, like us are permanent residents, mostly retired people.

There are a few surprises after we move in. Dennis finds out he has to fix the sewage line to the toilet. It wasn't installed properly and there's a sewage smell coming into the house. The old owner tried to tell him something is wrong but Dennis couldn't understand what he was trying to say. They also told us that the water heater worked "*mas o menos*", more or less. I find out that the pilot light goes out on windy days and usually in the middle of a shower.

Trying to live in such a small house is a challenge. Our house in Norway was far too big for two people. We spent so much time and money maintaining and cleaning rooms we never used. We did not want a big house again but fifty square meters[1] is really small. Dennis and I keep running into each other. We soon realize that we have to take turns being in the kitchen or bathroom. They are just too small for two people at the same time. We're glad that its springtime and we can be outside most the time. What will it be like in the winter? Our biggest problem right now is storage space. There's not a single storage closet. There is one small clothes closet in the bedroom barely big enough for the two of us. Our suitcases are stuffed with winter clothes and stored under the bed, as are our shoes and boots. We still have tools, sleeping bags, books, Christmas decorations and old documents that need to go somewhere, but where?

Our washing machine is under a fiberglass awning at the back of the house but otherwise it's exposed to the air. This is quite common here in Spain and works well in the summer. I don't like it much in the winter. During our first visit to the house in February the concrete was wet and growing mold, making it very slippery.

Every Saturday a loudspeaker blares on a truck that slowly cruises the neighborhood disturbing our peaceful mornings. We can't understand the words and wonder what it's all about.

One beautiful spring day it's warm and slightly overcast and perfect for working in the garden. While weeding, I once again hear a loudspeaker blaring far away. I listen to the announcement again and again as the truck slowly approaches. Then I begin to understand some words, "*refrigeradoras*", refrigerators, and "*lavadoras*", washing machines. I assume it's an advertisement; but as the truck nears I can see that it's a junk truck and that they are collecting old appliances. The next weekend we hear the word "*colchonés*", mattresses. This time it's a modern clean truck with an enclosed back and now they appear to be selling. What a strange way to do business.

We want to have a phone installed in the house. There has never been one and we notice that most of the homes in the *urbanización* don't have phones either. We stop at the *Telefonica* shop in *Lloret* and fill out papers to order one. When we give our address in an *urbanización* the clerk shakes his head and says there are always difficulties if you don't live in a *pueblo*. "They build streets like crazy and nothing is documented so the telephone company doesn't know where to go," he tells us. We explain, our street is twenty years old. It should be documented by

---

1.   about 500 square feet

now. He simply shakes his head. "If you don't have a phone in a week or two come back and see me."

Two weeks later, we return to the shop, still no phone. The clerk tells us we need to get a neighbor's phone number and give it to *Telefonica* so they can find our street in their records. A few days later we see our neighbor, one of the few with a telephone, opening his gate. We stop and introduce ourselves and try to explain in Spanish that we need his phone number to give to *Telefonica*. He agrees and writes it down for us.

Two weeks later we still have no phone. I call *Telefonica* to complain and am told that the order was cancelled because they could not find our house. I place a new order and tell them to please call and we can meet them at the entrance to the *urbanización* and show them the street.

Another two weeks go by and we still have no phone. One Saturday our neighbor yells at the gate and we go out to meet him. He tells us *Telefonica* called and has cancelled our order, they can't find the street. Why did they call him? I call *Telefoncia* again and place a new order. They say there is a backlog and we will have to wait twenty days.

Weeks later we have no phone. We don't know what to do but to keep trying so I call and place a new order.

Two weeks later, we have no phone. We have to make a trip to the states for a wedding. With our luck, *Telefonica* will come when we are out of town. I don't know whether to call and postpone the order until we return but decide not to bother. It will probably just complicate things and we'll never get a telephone.

I realize that I have taken so many things for granted. In America or Norway you can just call and order a telephone and the companies actually want to have your business. Here in Spain, they really don't care. If it's too much trouble they just throw away your order. We decide to ask our Spanish teacher if she knows how we can get a phone. We stumble through the story in Spanish, hoping she understands. She listens but just shakes her head. "It's a story I have heard many times."

We return from America and I call *Telefonica* again. They have cancelled my order once more and I ask them, "What can I do to get a telephone? I have tried so many times. I have been waiting three months." They promise to have a service man call us. To our surprise a service man appears at our gate the next day. Apparently we have fulfilled the mysterious but required waiting period and *Está!* we now have a telephone.

Slow Down

I can see our neighbor Pedro heading off into the woods every morning with his handmade machete. He tells us the machete is for the wild blackberry plants which he chops away as he walks. Some people like to eat the fruit but he doesn't bother, they are too much trouble. "*No me gustan, estan feo,*" he tells us, "I don't like them, they are ugly." They grab and poke at your legs and snag your clothes.

Pedro is one of the happiest people I have ever met. He's a little hard of hearing and greets us with a big loud '*buenas!*' every time we meet. He walks with a constant smile on his face even when carrying a large stack of wood on his shoulders, or hoeing in the garden. He tells me that he loves coming out here to this house and garden. During the week they live in Barcelona. His wife Louisa doesn't like to come out to the country as much as she used to. There's a new grandbaby at home and she wants to be near it.

I can't believe how friendly our neighbors are. They came to introduce themselves the moment they saw us, ask where we are from, how we like Spain, will we live here all year or just weekends? Every weekend they arrive with big smiles, walk over for a small chat often bringing us fruit and vegetables from their garden. One day we arrive home from a shopping trip and there is a plastic grocery bag filled with freshly dug plants hanging on our gate. I put them in pots, not knowing what they are and am pleasantly pleased a few weeks later with beautiful Black-eyed-Susan's.

Our moving truck arrived from Norway two days ago. The driver helped us to unload, which we didn't expect and were grateful for. We spoke Norwegian with him until we found out he was Irish and then we all switched to English. I am losing my Norwegian and was frustrated the other day when I could no longer count to ten. Spanish keeps getting in the way. When I really try hard then French numbers come up from some dark recesses of my mind. I haven't studied French for thirty years.

We've been unpacking and stacking what we don't have room for behind the house. There is a washing machine back there under a fiberglass awning. We will have to get rid of a nice sofa bed the old owners left and store most of our things under our bed. Their glassware and pots and pans will have to go too. Marta will take some of it for her rental house and the rest we leave near the recycling bins at the entrance of the *urbanización*. We stuff the sofa bed in the back of our car and tie the cushions on top then drive slowly down to the bins. There is a sign there for *"mobles"*, furniture. When we drive by after a few hours our sofa bed is already gone.

One cool sunny morning we decide to walk to a nearby hill. There's a little tower on the top. From there we expect to see *Maçanet*, the neighboring towns off *Hostalrich* and *Tordera*, as well as the Mediterranean Sea. The air is crisp and there are wild flowers blooming along the roadside. There are white daisies and wild blue and orange flowers that look like tiny forget-me-nots. A plant that I think is wild sage is budding out in purple flowers. I pinch off a leaf and crush it between my fingers but it's not aromatic. The wild fire last year has scarred this land. There are burnt tree trunks and branches lining the hillsides. In places, someone has cut down the charred stumps and stacked them in neat piles. Most of the cork oak trees have survived and are starting to bud out in grayish green leaves. The trunks are thick, gnarly and charred a deep black. We see a few people out collecting wild asparagus. The women are rolling it into bundles at the waistband of their aprons. The men balance it in the crook of their elbows. We try to look for it as we walk but can't spot any. I've grown asparagus in my garden so I know what it should look like but here with all the new plant life distracting me I just can't find any.

We are told the people here are crazy about wild mushrooms but we don't dare take any we see. I'm afraid of picking the wrong kind. I have a friend, a refugee from the war in Bosnia, who went through medical school there. She had to flee the country right in the middle of her internship. She warned me against the hobby. Every year one or two families were wiped out by eating bad mushrooms and their families always exclaimed—"we can't understand it, they were very experienced, they knew exactly which mushrooms were safe and which weren't." Apparently they didn't.

It starts to get warm as we reach the base of the final hill. There's a tiny goat path leading to the tower at the top. The *vistas* are wonderful. We can see far beyond the damages of the wildfire into the lush hills beyond. It always surprises me how green *Catalunya* is. In our imaginations, Spain had the dry brush land of *Andalucía* in the south, but here we see layer after layer of lush green hills. There is usually haze in the air, pollution or moisture from the sea (or both) which hide the mountains in the distance. Today, to the north, in the far distance, we can see the faint outline of the snowcapped Pyrenees.

I love the tempo of life here. People walk the streets in the evening, greeting each other or stand chatting in the road unhurried. They sit for hours in a restaurant with a cup of coffee or beer and read the paper or talk. Neither they nor the proprietor feel any urgency to pay the bill, to clear the table, to get ready for another guest. The people here seem to relax and enjoy life in a way that we have always been too busy to learn. We have a hard time slowing down. We tend to walk too fast, to hurry around people. We tap our feet when waiting in line and honk the horn when someone suddenly gets out of their car and leaves us waiting behind them in the street. When we finish eating, we have to get up and ask for the check. I wonder how long it will take us to learn to relax, to take things slow. Is it mental illness? We always seem to be in a hurry, but why? We have few deadlines here and nothing urgent. Here we have nothing to accomplish.

Getting Screwed

Our *nota simple* has arrived. It contains the property registration details for our house. We pour over them. There are diagrams of the construction and the plot. We quickly see that the house has just been given a permit to build. We find this so strange; the house has been finished for at least a year, but has just been given permission to be built.

We have managed to change the electricity to our name but we need to do the water. We hurry to *Maçanet* after Spanish class trying to make it to the water authority before they close. They are only open on Tuesdays for exactly two hours, from 11:00 to 1:00. The office is closed when we get there so we wait for a while. A woman soon comes to unlock the office; she explains that she was out for her morning coffee. We bring our huge piles of papers for the house plus our residence papers, not sure what documents they will need. She refuses to write down any information—we're not sure but we think she says it's the middle of the billing period so we must wait. Can we return in two weeks?

Two weeks later the same woman refuses to help us. Her computer is down so it's impossible for her to enter the data. Dennis asks; "Can you write it down on paper and enter it later?" She refuses. Can we return in two weeks?

Every two weeks we scramble after Spanish class to make it to the water office before it closes. After twelve weeks, her computer is still not working, and we still haven't paid a bill. I try to explain that we are living in the house but have not received a water bill. "*Vale, vale.*" She understands but what can she do? Then I ask if there is another place we can go? She tells us we can drive to *Santa Coloma de Farners*, but it is *fiesta* this week, perhaps next week? She writes down the address for us.

The water company in *Santa Coloma* refuses to put our name on the bill. "*Si, si,*" they can change the bank account so we can pay the bill-but the name, no. The name cannot be changed because the house has no *Licencia de Primera Ocupacion*, permission for occupancy. We look through our papers and find out that the building permit was good for three years. After that, we should apply for the occupancy permit.

Spain, with pressure from the European Union, is trying to catch up after decades of no housing regulation. The government uses the utility companies to enforce the laws, denying service to new housing that is illegally built. Dennis makes an appointment at the *ayuntamiento* or town hall of *Maçanet* for an inspector to look at our house. We are hopeful everything will be OK. We can't see any glaring problems that should stop an occupancy permit but we have heard so many horror stories about this permit that we are nervous. An older British couple had signed a contract to have a house built but as soon as the shell was completed, the builder stopped working and demanded more money. They of course refused to pay; they had a contract after all. But the builder refused to finish the house. They were able to finish enough of the interior themselves to be able to live there but they cannot get electricity or water connected because they do not have a *Licencia de Primera Ocupacion*. For three years, they have been sharing the neighbor's electricity, running an extension cord across the patio to the neighbor's house. Frustrated, not able to speak Spanish and out of money, they see no solution to their problem.

The inspector denies our occupancy permit. We have four infringements. The sidewalk in the front is not legal. It slopes down a few inches in front of the driveway and someone could trip and fall. He demonstrates this to us by walking down the sidewalk then flailing his arms and stumbling. He doesn't seem to notice that there is no sidewalk to the left or to the right of our house, or for that matter there is no other sidewalk on the entire street. Our laundry room is illegal. The fiberglass awning at the back of the house must be removed. Number three: the small bedroom is not on the house plans, there should only be one bedroom so the dividing wall has to go. Worst of all is the last item. The tiniest edge of the back corner of the house is about two feet too close to the property line. He measures from the corner to the wire fence and shows us with his hands: an arms length too close. We are shocked. What can we do? I try to convince him, "*No puede movear la Casa.*" We can't move the house. I don't know if I've used the right words, but he understands. He points to the lot next door. "*No se. Posible puede comprarse este parcela.*" I don't know, maybe you can buy that land. We're speechless.

After he leaves, we sit at the kitchen table in shock. We have just been screwed by Spanish real estate.

Poco Pee Pee

One of our cats is sick and I am worried about her. She tries to urinate and can't. She paces the floor leaving small drops of bloody urine. My cat book says that blockage of the urinary tract is a medical emergency. I try to call our English speaking veterinarian in *LLoret de Mar*. It's a Monday morning in May but he doesn't answer the office phone or his emergency number. I try for several hours with no luck. We finally decide to go to the vet in *Maçanet de La Selva*. We have never been there before. We don't expect them to speak English but we hope they speak Spanish, not just Catalan. We place the cat in her carrier and on the drive into town I look up the Spanish words for **urine infection** and **blockage**, trying to figure out how to explain her illness in Spanish.

The office is not busy so we are ushered right in to see the vet. He's a young man who thankfully speaks Spanish and a little English. I try to explain what is wrong with our cat but my mind goes blank even though I just looked up the words. Dennis tries to help but has the same problem. The doctor stops us and asks in broken English, "in the box, *poco* pee pee?" We both nod yes! That is exactly what we were trying to say. We are given medicine, special food and instructions for taking a urine sample. We return to the car. Dennis and I look at each other and smile. In unison we say; "*poco pee, pee*" and laugh. We've learned something from that doctor. Simple is best.

It's English

Teaching is going well although I have some days where I really make mistakes. I can't seem to explain things in a clear, concise way and I can see on the student's faces that they just don't understand.

They have trouble with pronunciation and want to know the rules. There are no rules for English pronunciation; or rather, there is an exception to every rule. I add some phonetics to the curriculum so they can at least read the dictionary. One of them gets frustrated when he learns that **woman** is pronounced:/wŏŏmn/ when it's singular but the plural **women,** is pronounced/wimin/. He insists on knowing why. I tell him "I don't know. It's English" but he is not satisfied. Why is the **k** in **knife** silent? Why don't you say the **gh** in **night** or in **through?** Then there is **enough**, and **tough**, where "**gh**" sounds like an "**f**" but **ghost** which has a completely different sound. My students teach me how hard English really is, often throwing their hands in the air in exasperation. They tell me Spanish is so much simpler. There are rules about pronunciation and you can trust them.

Sometimes I feel daunted by the huge job of teaching. I try to explain this to Marta, she's been teaching a long time and not just English, but French, German and Spanish. She says, "Don't worry. You should be grateful that your students can learn abstract ideas." She explains; "I have one student right now who simply can't grasp that a word might have another gender in a different language. He's learning German and I try to teach him that the word for window is masculine but he refuses to accept it. He says his mother taught him that window is feminine. Its *la ventana* not *el ventana* so it can't possibly be masculine, even in German. I try to tell him that it's just a language convention; that window, of course, isn't masculine or feminine but he refuses to accept it."

The language academy I work at has its own book and teaching method. In general, I like it but some of the curriculum seems ridiculous for beginners. They learn the words **vase** and **moose** in chapter two but have to wait for chapter fourteen to learn the days of the week. What's more important here? How often do we use the word moose? Who writes these books anyway? Have they ever tried to learn a new language?

I'm supposed to teach the expression **shall we**; for example, "**Shall we go to the movies?**" I would never say this and am tempted to drop it from my lesson plan or change it. I would say: "**Do you want to go to the movies**" or "**would you like to go to the movies?**" but never "**shall we**". The other teachers at the school are British so I discuss it with them. They claim, "Oh, yes—in British English we use **shall we** all the time. It's completely natural. I leave it in the lesson plan.

Dennis and I talk often about learning Spanish. He's better than I at forming sentences. He remembers words when he looks them up. I can look something up a hundred times in the dictionary and the next time I still can't remember it. I'm telling him about the verb *acercar*. It means to approach or come near. Why can't I remember this word? I'm reading a book in Spanish by Villlanonga about the murder of the Spanish poet Garcia Lorca. He uses this verb all the time and I just can't remember it. I leave a bookmark in the dictionary on this page so I can look it up over and over. Dennis tells me he uses word association to remember words. "*Acercar*, it's got the words *cerca* in it, you know that word, it means 'near'. So *acercar* means to come near." I try this trick with other words but it usually doesn't help me. I remember better by experience. When I had a terrible influenza and tried to explain to a doctor that I had a cough I mimed coughing. He told me the word for cough is *tos*. Now I have no trouble remembering that word. I often need things acted out.

I try to apply this to my teaching. Not everyone can just read and listen and learn. Some of us have to touch and feel and move to learn. My students probably think I'm just playing games but I make them stand and sit and run and jump when I teach them the verbs. Of course, they will read and write them too but maybe these little activities will help them remember.

Dennis complains about Spanish verbs. Each person singular and plural has a separate ending and then you have to think about whether to use the polite form or not. I tell him my students have the opposite problem, they think English is difficult because you can't tell who is speaking by the verb ending. All the verbs end alike. They ignore personal pronouns because they aren't needed in Spanish then all of a sudden they're important in English. Dennis says, "no matter what you say English is easier. Take a toolbox as an example. Spanish is like having millions of wrenches, one for each bolt ever made. English is like having a few wrenches that you use all the time and one adjustable one."

Time of the Flowers and Missing Russians

Our Spanish teachers have arranged a bus tour to the towns of *Girona* and *Besalu*. About forty people have signed up for the tour, a full day event starting at 8:30 in the morning and lasting until 8:00 in the evening. *Girona* is interesting at any time but this visit coincides with *Temp de Flores*, Time of the Flowers. It's a one week event held every year in May. I expect a normal flower show displaying roses, creative bouquets, the most exotic arrangement, etc. I am surprised by the exhibits, which are integrated with the buildings and gardens of the old town. Art and garden groups have made theme displays featuring life, birth, fairy tales and death. In addition to flowers, they have used odd assortments of materials making the displays curious, charming and sometimes odd. The day is cool and wet as we tromp through the puddles of the old town, ducking umbrellas. The guide is a young, wiry man who carries a giant yellow sunflower on top of a long stick so the group can find him through the crowds. I have difficulty understanding his descriptions of the displays through the noise of the rain, people talking in various mother tongues and his fast, soft spoken Spanish.

One display is of large white daisies hanging on an old stone wall. But these aren't real daisies. Each one is at least a meter across. There are fifteen or twenty of these *flowers* scattered across the stone wall. Some of the petals are hollow like donuts and some are solid. The title of the piece is written on the wall in Catalan; "*m'estima, no m'estima.*" I notice some of the petals are gone. It dawns on me that the theme is, he loves me or he loves me not. As I take a closer look, the yellow center of these flowers are bouquets of real daisies but the white petals are toilet seats and lids.

There's another flower display symbolizing our journey toward death, hundreds of black umbrellas are stuck in the earth and rocks lining a turbulent brook, they are interspersed with red roses. Fog rises from underneath the umbrellas. I try to capture it on film.

We enter an old building and the cave like walls are hung with mirrors completely covered in pink and green pastel carnations. It's strikingly beautiful, the contrast of the hard cold stone walls, against the soft, pastel flowers.

There is a retired Italian couple, Marianna and Enrico, who sit behind us in our morning Spanish class. They have always been very friendly and today we learn that they have lived in South Africa and America and speak English very well. Marianna helps explain what the guide is saying, she understands him better than I. At the end of the day we see an interesting exhibit of tin sheets cut into two dimensional cactus shapes topped with spiked pink and green flowers. Enrico becomes very excited and tells us the flowers are from South Africa, the only place in the world where they grow. I think the sight of them has made him a little home sick. He waves his arms and raves about what a wonderful place Johannesburg was to live, and that it is now ruined, ruined by Mandela and his government. "It's not a nice place anymore," he tells us shaking his head in disgust. I'm surprised because he's the only person I have ever heard say a negative word about Nelson Mandela.

The rain has stopped and the clouds have disappeared. Umbrellas are stowed and with the sun shinning, we soon start removing rain jackets and sweaters. Our walk continues and there are many, many more displays. Near lunchtime, Dennis and I are very hungry and lose the little ability we had to concentrate on Spanish so we wander and look hardly listening to the guide. Nonetheless, we are very impressed, it is more creative and exotic than we ever expected.

We are given thirty minutes of free time in *Girona* before we are supposed to meet back at the bus and go to lunch. Dennis and I buy some bottled water and potato chips to eat and look in some shop windows. Finally, we board the bus. We are thirty minutes late leaving as some of the students don't return to the bus on time. The teachers have to get off the bus and search for them. Two British students apologize as they get on the bus, saying they got lost.

We then head for *Besalu* and lunch. *Besalu* is a quaint medieval town north and east of *Girona*. With a population of about two thousand, its main industry is tourism. The town has a famous fortified Roman bridge. However, the bridge is very unusual. Normally Roman bridges are symmetrical with even arches and long straight expanses. This bridge has uneven arches and is bent in the middle. No one knows the architect or the reason for the anomaly.

The town also has two interesting Romanesque churches with stark, austere interiors and a newly discovered Jewish ritual bath from the 12th century. The bath, discovered by accident and the only one in Spain, has been declared a historical treasure.

Today the town is nearly empty of tourists except for our group. After disembarking, we head directly for the restaurant and a *menu del dia*, which has been pre-ordered.

Marianna and Enrico sit next to us. We are joined by a Russian woman from our Spanish conversation class and a woman from Holland who speaks English. We eat and talk in a mixture of English and Spanish about the food, living in Spain and learning Spanish. We answer and ask the usual question, "Why are you in Spain?" As we eat our salad I ask Marianna, "Is it normal that salad is always served with oil and vinegar? We've lived here six months and never had any other kind of salad dressing." She tells me yes, for southern Europeans, they like it pure; oil and vinegar is the way to eat salad. "When I lived in America they had many different salad dressings. I think they are strange. I don't like them."

Marianna hardly touches the first course, a large plate of rigatoni pasta and meat sauce. She says the pasta is overcooked. "I'm Italian, I can't eat this pasta." I am too hungry to care and think the pasta is good anyway. Enrico brags that Marianna is a very good cook. She confirms that yes, she makes nice sauces but she just doesn't like to spend time in the kitchen anymore. The Dutch lady next to me laughs and says, "I like that—someone who feels just like me," as she lifts her glass of wine in a toast.

The main course is chicken, cooked perfectly tender swimming in a delicious sauce with wild mushrooms. Dennis eats three helpings of chicken. We are served *crema catalana* for desert, which we all agree we like very much. This is not a good example of the dessert. It is served cold instead of warm. The top, which should be a golden bitter caramelized sugar, is barely brown. We exit the restaurant quickly after lunch and take a much-needed walk through town.

We walk the entire length of the town in about fifteen minutes then wander the back streets looking at the few houses and gardens. We meet back with the group and take tours of the two churches and the Jewish bath. Near the end of the day we sit inside the Jewish bath listening to the guide describe the ritual cleansings that were performed here with water exchanged constantly from the nearby river. A British woman comments aloud that she doesn't understand anything. The guide politely repeats the talk in English, which of course is only beneficial to a few of us. I see one of our Spanish teachers shaking her head in disappointment. Then we walk the Roman bridge taking photos and it is time to leave.

Back on the bus, six people are missing. About thirty minutes later the same two British people who were late in *Girona* get back on the bus and apologize, "Sorry, sorry," they say, "we got lost." I find it hard to believe, not just because they used the excuse earlier today but, how can you get lost in a town that can be walked in fifteen minutes? We can't leave yet because four students are still missing. The driver makes a loop from one end of the town to the other and we all watch out the windows of the bus. The teachers finally get off the bus and walk through the town looking. Eventually they come back, alone. They are getting worried. Dennis and I are sitting behind them in the bus and I hear their discussion:

"We should leave. They are adults. They knew to come back here."

"Maybe something has happened, we should call the police."

"They are worse than children."

They decide to call the police but are told nothing can be done. The students are adults and have not been missing long. The teachers ask around the bus if anyone knows the phone numbers of the missing. Nobody does. We sit and wait and people are beginning to get annoyed. Finally, one woman says maybe she can try to find out their phones number by calling some friends. After a few phone calls, they are finally found. The four young Russians decided to take a taxi home. They are in *Lloret de Mar*. We are all shocked. Not only would it cost a fortune for a one and a half hour taxi ride, but why didn't they tell anyone?

An hour and a half later, we roll into *Lloret de Mar* only to be stopped by the highway police, *Mossos*. They want to inspect the bus. Everyone lets out a collective groan at the delay. We all slump in our seats, weary from this long day and resigned to yet another delay.

Coffee with Marta

Marta visits me for coffee and croissants one morning. We sit outside enjoying the sun in the cool spring weather. She is wearing a thick winter jacket and has to take it off after the sun warms her back. She tells me a little about the kids and their school studies and we talk about teaching.

The construction workers next door turn on their radio. It's blaring so loud we have to raise our voices to talk. Marta jumps out of her chair and goes next door and yells at them to turn the music down. I tell Marta that compared to Norwegians the Spanish are incredibly loud people.

"For example, if you are waiting for a train in the center of Oslo, at one of the busiest stations in the whole country, it's so quiet you can hear a pin drop. There is no place that quiet in the whole of Spain. We assume that Norwegians have learned to keep their mouths shut just to keep their teeth warm."

Marta laughs.

I'm only half joking. I've experienced the inside of my nose freezing in the winter and on some cold winter days my teeth would throb from the cold.

"They are really noisy here," she agrees. "They are strange though. They can be very rude with noise but very considerate in other ways.

I used to live in this apartment and one young man used to irritate me so much. He would sit on his motorcycle on the street outside my apartment and make all kinds of noise with the engine. No matter how many times I asked him to stop, he kept doing it repeatedly. Then one day I am on the balcony watering my plants. I'm talking to a woman who lives in the apartment across the road who is also on her balcony. She wasn't old but looked like it. She told me that her hair suddenly turned white the day she learned that her son was killed in a motorcycle accident. While we were talking her doorbell rings and she can't see who it is from her balcony, so she asks me to look for her since I have a better view of the entrance. It was that young man, the one who makes all the noise with his motorcycle and he had a big bunch of red roses in his arms. She smiles at me and tells me, 'he was my son's friend and it was a year ago today that my son died.'

No matter what else you think about the Spanish you must admit they are thoughtful to old people and children. That makes up for a lot."

I think about what Marta has just told me. It's true that I have been surprised at how the men here love children. It is often the men walking their children home from school at lunch and playing with them in the park. Not only the dads but also teenagers seem to love children too. They always stop and tease them and play with them, even on a busy street or in a supermarket. I can't imagine that happening in America or Norway where it would definitely be uncool.

I change the subject and ask Marta to tell me about how she and Carlos met. She had been promising to tell me.

"Oh, that's quite a story. Do you really want to hear it?"

I'm very interested but don't want to pry, "yes, but only if you want to tell it."

"Well, I was teaching a course in Flemish for some hotel employees. It was just a short three-week course, just to teach them some basics. Most of the students were women but there was this one man, he was so good. Even with difficult pronunciation every word I taught came right back out of his mouth, perfectly. He had a very good ear for languages and was so smart. He also had this bright, alive look in his eyes that was very attractive. It reminded me of my children's father.

I guess I have to tell you about my children's father before I can tell you about Carlos. I was living in this house in *Sitges*. The neighbor down there was this very attractive single man. He was so clever and articulate. He was very open and had this light in his eyes. We became friends, not romantic, just friends. He really had a problem with women. He just used them and threw them away. I used to tell him that it wasn't right. He got a seventeen-year-old girl pregnant. He didn't want to marry her. I felt sorry for her because she had such a difficult life. Her mother was a prostitute so she'd really had it hard. I really stuck up for that girl and now they are married with another baby. Anyway, we were friends and I was getting to be 36 years old and I thought if I'm going to have a baby I have to do it soon. I wasn't seeing anyone so I just asked this neighbor if he would do it—if he would be the father of my children. He thought about it for a while then he said yes. We were friends after the children came too. He helped me move from *Sitges* when I bought an apartment in *Blanes*. I was even friends with his wife when they got married because she knew I had stood up for her before.

Well, back to Carlos. I was teaching him in this class and I was very interested in him so I looked up his registration card to find out a little more about him. He was single but he was fourteen years younger than me. Then I knew that I had to just forget him, fourteen years is too much. Well, the class went on and one day during a break he starts telling me about a film that he had seen. Then we find out we have the same interest in old films and books. A few days later he tells me he is going to another old film on the weekend with some friends and would I like to join them? I'm not sure how to take this, is it a date or just some friends together? Anyway, I am busy so I have to say no. The whole time I'm telling myself not to get interested in him. On the last day of class, only Carlos shows up. He explains that the other students, the women, work in housekeeping and they had to work extra today so they won't be coming. We try to have a class but with just the two of us, we decided to go for coffee. Well one thing led to another and…"

Marta's voice drifts off and then she laughs:

"Well that was how we got together. The strange thing is that he always reminded me of my children's father and he had the same last name too. I didn't think too much about that though because it's a common name. There are many people with that name in this area. One day when we were first together, I told Carlos that he really reminded me of this other man and Carlos asked his name. When I told him we both got such a shock. Carlos is the stepbrother of my children's father."

I'm so shocked I'm almost speechless. "And you had no idea that they were related?"

"No. In this big country I just happen to find two men from the same family. It was really difficult for us. Carlos didn't want to tell his family. I finally decided to tell them. I didn't want them finding out from someone else. They were pretty upset in the beginning but now they've accepted it. I don't see the children's father anymore. It makes Carlos feel strange. They're not really friends. Carlos never knew his real father and his mother married and divorced his step dad within a few years. The boys didn't even live together that long when they were growing up."

"Wow, I tell her. You could write a book about your life."

The End of Classes

Our Spanish class ended today. We had a potluck breakfast for the last day of class. The students brought juice, coffee and something to eat, plus a little to share. There are croissants and cookies, cakes, donuts and chocolates. I made a small cinnamon cake and it disappears fast. Some girls from India bring chai to drink. Everyone is friendly on the last day of class, even students I've never spoken to come to ask if I will be returning for the autumn classes. Natalia, a Russian woman, corners me for a good part of the morning and tells me her story. She was a medical doctor in Russia. She's divorced, and now is living here with a Spanish boyfriend. The only work she can find (illegally) is cleaning houses. She's about forty years old, with short curly dark hair. She has a raspy, gruff voice but a gently quality about her. She's speaking to me in a mixture of English and Spanish. Her Spanish is much better than mine and I have a hard time following her conversation, especially over the din of the other students chatting. She asks for my phone number-she would like to practice English over the summer. I'm happy to give it to her, I think the summer will be lonely for me and I would like another friend.

It's also my last week of teaching English. I've given my students two practice exams to prepare them for the final exam. They need to get 50% correct in order to continue to the next level. They both do miserably on the practice exams. I know how easy it is to make errors on these tests. I did miserably on my Spanish exam, but if they fail I feel it reflects on me as a teacher.

We drill and drill basic grammar points: how to form questions, using **who, what, where, when and why** but also using **do**. We practice using the correct form of verbs and the prepositions: **at, by, in, on**. We practice telling time, introductions and greetings, asking prices, describing daily routines; everything that will be on the final exam. One section is an individual oral exam. I will ask simple questions and listen to their answers. They are relieved that I will be giving the oral exam and not another teacher. They are used to my voice and my American accent, which will make it easier.

I'm excited and nervous for them on the day of the test. They both do the exam quickly, too quickly, I feel, and I press them to recheck their answers. They have trouble with the listening section. They have to listen to a dialog on a tape and answer questions. The speakers on the tape have heavy British accents and they have to listen, read and answer questions all at the same time. I know it's very difficult but I'm only allowed to play the tape twice. They are both shaking their head in disgust as they hand in the exam. I glance through them quickly, spying the mistakes.

The last day of English classes, I bring cookies and juice to celebrate. Both of them have passed their tests with approximately 70 percent correct. I'm thrilled for them. We review the test and learn some basic food vocabulary while we eat and drink. They thank me for the food and the class and we shake hands and say goodbye. I wish them luck. I've already decided not to teach here again in the autumn. I'll try to find a school closer to home but I feel sad to not see them again.

Summer Arrives and Mom Falls

It's been cool and rainy all spring. We are still using heaters at night to keep the house comfortable. Where is sunny Spain? Have we picked the right place to live? Suddenly at the end of May the temperatures rise and the sun comes out and it's beautiful. Flowers start blooming everywhere and there is so much pollen around that it looks like frost on the ground in the mornings. Plant vendors have arrived at the weekly markets selling small seedlings of squash, artichokes, peppers, cucumber, melon and pumpkin. There are herb plants too, basil and parsley, mint, oregano, and huge bundles of spring onions. I'm not sure if these are for planting or eating. Would someone really plant forty or fifty spring onions? As I walk through our neighborhood, I see that the answer is yes. They plant in abundance here. There are rows and rows of pole beans, each garden having thirty or forty plants. I plant three pole bean plants every year and we always have more than we can eat. What will they do with all those beans?

One warm afternoon we walk down to the local shop to buy ice cream. They've installed an outdoor bar and patio. There are four *boules* courts next to the patio and today there is a lively game going with lots of spectators talking and cheering. An outdoor stereo system is blasting music and we have to shout to order our ice creams. The kitchen is open and smells of wonderful fried onions and peppers. Walking home, eating our ice cream we peek through fences as we walk to see the flowers and vegetables. At one house six old people are gathered around a picnic table, all talking at the same time, all shelling beans and waving their hands in the air. No need to even watch what they are doing, I think they must have done this all their lives.

When we arrive home, Pedro, from across the street, brings me tomato plants. I bought four plants at the market last week and he is giving me eight more. I'm thrilled to take them and thank him very much. What will we do with all those tomatoes?

There are three terraces next to the driveway at the entrance to our house. One is filled with rose bushes. They have some disease of black spots and a rusty powder. I know nothing about roses, but hope to save them. I cut them back, removing nearly every leaf, hoping to stop the disease. I find strong balls of roots in the

94

ground as I'm preparing the vegetable garden and don't know if they are weeds or something planted by the old owners. I throw most of them over the fence but plant some in the flowerbed next to the roses.

The middle terrace will be my vegetable garden and it will be small; two zucchini, two squash, one pumpkin, a cucumber, four bean plants, four sweet peppers, eight leeks and a small bed of carrots. Oh yes, and twelve tomato plants.

I plant ice plant in the top terrace. It's sandy there, and we want something low that won't block the view coming out of the driveway. Ice plant does wonderfully here; it tolerates the heat and dry season and seems to choke out weeds as well. Along the fence near the road I have to chop and dig and pull to get the weeds out. They have roots deep into the soil and I can't reach them because there are dead charred tree stumps interfering. I don't have the energy to remove the tree trunks this year. I can tell this area will be my problem child this year.

Juan, one of our neighbors, stops by to say hello. Always looking for gardening advice I ask if it is too late to plant *patatas*, potatoes. You have to do it in March he tells me. Eyeing my newly weeded garden, he adds that I need to use *estiercol*. He asks if we have seen anybody strange last week. His eggs were stolen from the hen house. He's very agitated telling us about it and waves his arms in the air. He's had chickens here for fourteen years and never had a problem. Who would steal his eggs? Dennis says it must have been someone who was hungry. Juan also tells us the neighbors up the street had their TV stolen. We're disappointed to hear this. Theft is a huge problem in Spain. We hear stories of it all the time. What a shame, it has reached our little community.

After the garden is cleaned up and planted, I invite Marta to bring her mom over for a look. Her mom has been visiting for the winter to help Marta with the kids while Carlos is away. Her mom helped us look through real estate catalogues for houses so I know she would like to see what we bought.

It's a beautiful spring day when Marta and her family arrive. They are bundled up in coats but soon remove them and sit in lawn chairs on the porch. Marta's daughter, Elise has brought a soccer ball and has soon enticed Dennis into a kicking game. Jon heads down to the creek below our house, and we can see him swinging on branches near the water. Elise soon forgets the soccer game and joins her brother and Dennis flops into a chair relieved. I give Marta and her mom a small tour. The house is so small it only takes a few minutes. We sit and have coffee outside then Marta calls the kids. They come running up the hill through the brush and when they emerge Marta is horrified to see they are black from head to toe from soot, the remains of last year's wildfire. "I just did laundry and they were supposed to wear those clothes to school tomorrow," she tells me.

Elise runs ahead to the car then turns around and kicks her soccer ball down to us. Marta's mom sees it coming and seventy years young, tries to kick it back. Our driveway slopes to the right and she loses her balance. As if in slow motion I see her fall backwards. I'm standing right next to her but am paralyzed and can't react. She tries to catch herself with her hands and throws them behind her then lands with a thud on the concrete flat on her back. I'm terrified she has hit her head. She doesn't move. Frozen, horrified, I am afraid she's dead. Then she moans and we all scramble to help. She doesn't want to move. She tells Marta that she can't see; that everything is black. Marta translates for us. Does she have a concussion? After a few minutes, we help her get up. I stand behind her and lift her from her armpits. I run to the front of the house and grab a lawn chair for her to sit on. I don't know if she can walk. Marta runs to her car and grabs some fruit and puts a slice of orange in her mother's mouth. I'm not sure why. I offer water, but she just wants to sit. Marta translates for me. "She says her hand hurts, but her vision is coming back." I feel so bad and so helpless. I don't know what to do. Should we call an ambulance? She shakes her head no; she just wants to sit for a minute. I replay her fall in my head, wishing I could have caught her. If I'd stepped forward one step she could have fallen against me instead of on the ground. Why didn't I?

Later that night I ring Marta to find out how her mom is. They had to go to the hospital because her arms were hurting. She has broken both forearms, one is just a crack but the other is a real break. Luckily, there's no concussion. She's on pain medication now, but has two casts on her arms. We offer to pay for the doctor bill or for the medicine, but Marta refuses. The emergency room is free and the doctor was an old student of hers and gave her the medicine no charge. She won't be going home soon though. There is no way she can travel by herself with two broken arms.

Jon's Birthday, Tourists and Missing Bidets

Marta invites us to her son's birthday party in June. Children are coming to play with him but she wants some friends to join her for lunch. We arrive on a cloudy Saturday afternoon. Marta has set up a table on the veranda. This is the first overcast day in a month and we all look forward to the possibility of rain, although Marta is not happy that it happened just today. Her kids run back and forth surrounded by their four dogs and disappear around the end of the house. Her mom has got her casts off and gone back to the Netherlands. Carlos has returned from Andorra and they are back together again. Marta tells us it's going well. Carlos found a job at a four-star hotel in *Lloret de Mar*. The only difficult thing is that he has to work the night shift, midnight to 8:00 in the morning. I ask Carlos how he likes his job. He tells me, "It's OK. The hotel is not very nice. Well, it's four-star, but now it's broken in many places. We Spanish, when we found out we could make money from tourists we build nice hotels and they come and give us lots of money. We don't know how to think business. We are so happy to have money. We spend it all on car, wine, food. We have fun. The hotel needs money too, but we don't think about it. Tourists come and they pay but soon the hotel does not look so nice. The new people, the young ones, they are better. They begin to understand how to make business. They want, not one hotel, but three, four, ten hotels. They know how to make money and to make the hotel stay nice."

We eat olives and peanuts while we wait for lunch. Carlos opens a bottle of red wine. I ask him if he likes working nights. "It must be difficult."

"It's OK," he shrugs his shoulders. There's not much work at night. But I feel strange sometimes. If someone ask me am I tired, I say, 'I don't know.' Maybe yes, maybe no. Maybe I am always tired."

Marta has made *gazpacho*, the popular Spanish cold tomato soup. "Carlos says this is not real *gazpacho*." Marta tells us, "I put apples in it." Authentic or not, it's delicious. She has also made whole-wheat croutons and we are silent as we enjoy the soup. The dogs tire of chasing the children and try to join us on the porch but Carlos is firm with them. "*Afuera!*" Out! They obey instantly.

I remark, "You're good with the dogs."

"Well, I walk with them, and I give them food." He tells me, "Dogs are like Germans, give them clear rules and they are happy."

It's such a strange thing to say that I start laughing.

"It's true." He explains, "At the hotel I can tell the Germans, 'First you, then you, then you...' and they stand and wait, they are happy. They will stand and wait for hours even. I can't do that with Spanish or French. They don't care what I say. They all want to be first. But if you don't give the rule to the German then you get big trouble." He raises his arms and ducks his head as if to protect himself. "Big trouble."

We tell Marta and Carlos about a show we watched on TV. There was a camera placed in a third floor window of an apartment block somewhere in Russia or Eastern Europe. It was focused on the street below right in front of the apartment building. There was no dialog, in fact, no sound at all, just the film from the camera. They filmed three years in the life of a huge pothole in the street in front of the apartment block. Workmen come and tear up the street and repair it over and over and over again. The seasons change, rain, snow, wind, sun. People walk by with groceries and dogs. Children run and dogs sniff the ground. In the winter, people shovel snow, in the spring they wash the building and sidewalk and sweep debris into the gutter, and the whole time, over and over, workmen tear up the street and repair it again and again. We were mesmerized.

Marta thinks it must have been Russia. "They have the most terrible plumbing problems. "I had a friend from Russia. She said when her apartment building in St. Petersburg was inspected they would make the inspector wait after each floor, so they could remove the sinks and toilets and install them on the next floor so the inspection could continue."

Carlos tells us about at incident that happened at a hotel where he worked. "One of the cleaning girls came to the front desk and said that a bidet was missing from one of the rooms. The manager had not ordered repairs so they checked the room and then soon discovered that twelve rooms all from the same floor were missing bidets. They looked on the computer and saw that a Russian tour group had just checked out so they ran outside and stopped the bus. They made them open the storage area under the bus and there were the twelve missing bidets!"

Marta has made three salads, rice with nuts and fruit, potato with olive oil and egg salad. Everything is fresh and delicious and we talk about music and books and politics. Carlos says that he can't understand why there is so little political debate in the United States. "In Spain," he says, "the government does one thing and everyone is always asking questions and pressing, 'Is it the right thing to do?' Even after it's over, we look back and ask 'was it right?' But in the United States, no one questions. The government does one thing and claims it is correct. No one is asking, 'Is it the right thing to do?' If they do ask then maybe they get in trouble, get called names or other bad things" We shake our heads in agreement. It wasn't always this way but now it seems true to us too and we don't know why.

The Emergency Room and Depression

The weather has turned hot and dry. There is no rain during May and June, not a cloud in the sky. At first, we love it, after the cold wet winter and spring. After the first month, however we begin to tire of the relentless sun. The crops in the field are already turning golden and the wildflowers and weeds are setting seed and drying up. It's hazy nearly every day and from our front porch we can barely see the outline of the mountain of *Montnegre*.

People are arriving in our *urbanización* daily. Houses that have been closed all winter are now open. There's the sound of suburbia on the weekends; weed eaters, motorcycles, all terrain vehicles, barbeques and birthday parties, stereos blaring rap, disco, flamenco and Spanish folk music. The restaurant at the entrance of the *urbanización* is open and serving *menu del dia* everyday. There are cars parked along the narrow streets and dogs barking everywhere, constantly, day and night. Dennis tells me that cement mixers and barking dogs are the sounds of Spain.

Construction crews are working harder than ever. Someone is preparing a lot for a new house down the block. For weeks, we've listened to the sound of a heavy machine hammering away at a solid rock. This week, to add to the noise, three men arrive with chain saws and weed eaters to clear the lots surrounding our property. They work from 8:00 in the morning to 8:00 at night with just a few long breaks in the middle of the day. The whining and pounding and roar of the motors are relentless and after a while, we are pacing the house from agitation. To escape the noise, we decide to go to *Lloret de Mar* for coffee and a pastry and to sit near the beach and watch the ocean. We know a spot on a rocky hill where we can sit on benches in the cool shade.

In the summer Spaniards escape to *las costas,* the coasts of Spain, to flee the intense heat of the interior of the country. People have started to arrive in *Blanes, Tossa de Mar* and *LLoret de Mar* by droves. On the weekends the motorway to *Tossa de Mar* is backed up all the way to *Vidreres*, thirty kilometers away. *LLoret de Mar* has a flat sandy beach at the end of the tourist district. Today it is packed with people sunbathing. There are advertisements for boat tours and parasailing. People are snorkeling near the rocks on either end of the sandy beach. The city streets are crowded with people speaking Spanish, German, French and Russian. The northern European tourists are scantily clad, bright red skin bulging out of skimpy bathing suits. They wear swimsuits everywhere, not just at the beach but in the shops and restaurants too. Everywhere we see people eating ice cream, candy bars, baguette sandwiches and bags of chips. Businesses that have been closed since we moved here are open and thriving.

Months ago Marta recommended a *patisserie* that sits in a small square off the main shopping street of *Lloret*. It's usually not crowded and it's quiet. Plus, she told us that when the country converted from *pesetas* to euros two years ago, most businesses took the opportunity to raise prices. The exchange rate was set at 165 pesetas to 1 Euro. If a cake cost 165 pesetas, instead of setting the price to 1 Euro, they set it to 1.65 Euro. Thankfully, this café did not do it, and their prices are very reasonable. Today there are no tables available so we order pastries to go and head straight to our favorite spot on the rocky cliff to sit in the shade and enjoy the view. The benches are full of sunburned tourists and with difficulty; we find another place to sit.

My husband is perfectly happy by himself but I feel so isolated. We rarely see Marta and Carlos since they are both working full time. Our neighbors are friendly but I simply don't have the words to carry on anything but the simplest conversation. They mostly just wave and smile and yell, "*Bon Dia!*"

I've had a small chronic rash on my inside elbow and on my neck for almost a year. I've tried all kinds of creams and lotions and herbal remedies including basil and aloe. Nothing helps and it's very itchy. I've been to three different doctors in Norway. The first doctor recommended antihistamines, cortisone cream and when those failed, a dermatologist. The dermatologist recommended sunbathing and moisturizer. That didn't help at all. The third doctor recommended steroid tablets but they make my joints swell up and there's no change in the rash. I've been taking antihistamines for almost a year but the small rash doesn't heal. Since we moved to Spain, I've tried acupuncture. The doctor is Chinese and is so relaxed, I feel calmer just being around him. He has an office in *Blanes*, speaks to me in a mixture of Spanish and English and writes in Chinese. I've enjoyed the acupuncture treatments but the rash refuses to go away.

This summer my rash explodes. I don't know if it's pollen or the heat or what but it now reaches from my elbows to my chin and covers the top of my shoulders and underarms and shoulder blades. It itches and burns and I feel I'll go mad from the itching. I want to tear my skin off and let it grow back new. I stop at the pharmacy and show them the rash, asking if they can recommend something. The young woman behind the counter fetches an older woman from the back room. The older woman recoils when she sees it then shakes her head; "*necesita un medico*" she tells me; "you need a doctor." I don't have a doctor here and am not sure how to find one. I'm desperate and Dennis drives me to the emergency room at the hospital in *Blanes*.

I check in at the emergency room and wait about fifteen minutes to see a doctor. Two women in green surgical gowns interview me in a small room off the waiting room. One of them is in training and the other one explains everything as she examines me. She takes my temperature by sticking a thermometer in my armpit and asks me questions about my general health. Then they ask me what is wrong and I lift up my arms and take off my t-shirt. They both pull back and suck in their breath when they see my rash. I have the skin of a ruby red Gila monster. When I pulled off my shirt I forgot about the thermometer in my armpit and it goes flying to the floor and shatters. We all stare at it and I apologize profusely. The nurse pats me on the arm and says, "*tranquile, tranquile,*" relax, relax.

They take me to an examination room to see the doctor. He steps in and looks and says he thinks it's an allergic reaction and then leaves. A nurse comes in and takes blood, gives me an injection and sets up an IV in my arm. I lay for ages on the table, listening to the sounds around me. An elderly man is rolled on a gurney into the room next to mine. Doctors are asking him in Spanish and English, "Did you fall. Did you hurt your head?" But he doesn't seem to respond because they ask repeatedly. I hear another doctor speaking German to a little girl and her mother. With the IV in one of my arms, I can't scratch so I twist and turn trying to ease the itching with one hand. I doze on and off waiting for something to happen. After a while, the nurse returns and asks if I have family waiting. I tell her my husband is in the waiting room. A few minutes later Dennis walks in and asks if I'm OK. The nurse fetched him so he could sit with me. I'm grateful for the company but wish they would tell me what I'm waiting for. They must be doing some blood tests. We wait for another hour. The doctor returns and tells me, it was definitely allergies. I will have to find a permanent doctor who can advise me. He gives me an injection and prescription for more antihistamines. The nurse returns to remove the IV and says we can leave.

I don't know what to do. The doctors couldn't help me with cortisone. I've spent hundreds of euros on salves and creams and antihistamines. I meet a friend of Marta's who had a problem with allergic eczema and got help from a homeopathic doctor. I decide to try one instead of going back on cortisone tablets.

I ask at the pharmacy in *Lloret* if there is a homeopathic doctor in the city and they recommend one. He works at a private medical clinic. He's young and extremely handsome, very warm and energetic. This worries me. I think I'd feel more comfortable with someone old and cranky, someone experienced. He does speak English though; his mother is British and his father is Basque.

He gives me a long interview and then puts me on a strict diet to eliminate the possibility of food allergies and gives me a prescription for lots of vitamins and some tablets to cleanse my liver. He tells me to do the cleansing for six weeks then we will start the homeopathic treatment.

The diet is difficult; no gluten, no sugar, no dairy, no red meat, no caffeine, no alcohol but I am willing to try it to get rid of this rash. After six weeks, there is little change. The doctor starts me on a homeopathic program, three types of medicine to change the ph of my skin. He tells me he's treated thirty or forty people with rashes but he has never seen anyone with one so gigantic. I'm not happy to be the exception here. He also tells me skin problems are difficult and often are slow to heal but I should notice some reduction in the itching soon. I'm hopeful.

Four weeks later, I've spent hundreds of euros on vitamins, homeopathic medicines and doctor visits and have not improved. The rash still itches like crazy. The skin is painful, every time I move my arm or shift position there are sharp stinging pains. I can't sleep at night because the itching and pain keep me awake. I have some old cortisone tablets left so I start taking them again. They don't help at all.

I call my doctor and tell him I'm going mad. He increases my homeopathic dosage and gives me some additional medicine. I can hardly leave the house. Moving is painful. Sweating makes me itch even worse. I don't want to see anyone, talk to anyone. I don't want to write. The weather is hot and I sit in front of the fan all day just to keep from sweating. I have to force myself to get up and cook lunch. I dread even those small movements. I try to distract myself with reading books and watching movies. I meditate and watch the pain and itching. I find at times I can detach and just watch it. It helps but I can't maintain the concentration. Other times I pace the house—desperately trying not to scratch but giving in to it anyway, then suffering as the rash leaks yellow lymphatic fluid or bleeds. Scabs form and then the itching begins again. Like any person who has suddenly become ill, I want my old life back; my life before this misery. We're on a very strict budget and since I'm not working this summer, I worry about the money I'm spending on medicine and doctors. The medicine doesn't help. I have some good days when I feel a little better, a little less pain, a little less itching but I look at myself in the mirror and I know I am not healing.

Visitors, Dali and No Meat, Please!

We have friends visiting from England who are looking for property to buy. They have started a company that builds ecological houses made of earth bag, cob, and straw bales. They have bought land in Poland, Hungary, and Russia and now they are interested in Spain. We fetch them on a rainy Monday morning in early July. The drive to *Girona* airport is only thirty minutes and the airport is almost empty when we arrive.

It's good to see Galvin and Barbara again. We have known Galvin for years but do not know his Russian wife Barbara very well. They married in a whirlwind two years ago after a short Internet courtship and an even shorter two-week face-to-face meeting. Their marriage hasn't been easy but they are still together and seem happy enough. We are all excited as we pile into the car and drive back to *Maçanet*. They will only be in Spain three days and want to start looking at land immediately but first they want breakfast. They had a cheap no frills flight from Newcastle and desperately need some caffeine. We stop in a local bar in *Maçanet* for coffee and pastries. The room is long and narrow with tables on the right and the bar running lengthwise down the left side. It already reeks of cigarette smoke even this early in the morning. There is a TV blaring in the far corner. Women are chattering away at a nearby table. I have to yell over the noise to order coffee at the bar. When the espresso machine is added to the noise the din is incredible. I try to explain to our friends that if they live in Spain they have to get used to noise, but they can't hear what I'm saying.

There are several real estate agents in this small town and we look in all the windows and stop to ask if they have land for sale. They all say yes but tell us we have to make an appointment for later in the day or for tomorrow. We make one appointment for the afternoon and one for tomorrow then drive to *Vidreres* to ask the agent who sold us our house if she has anything available. I called her a week ago and asked if the vacant property next to our house is for sale and she promised to check on it. She's very busy when we arrive. Every sentence is interrupted by a telephone call that she apparently has to take. What a contrast to the winter months when we could take all the time we wanted to chat. She finally explains that the property next to ours is part of a group of twenty lots and not for sale. She has one lot available in our *urbanización* and gives us the map and directions. The price is twice as high as I expect; it's nearly doubled since we were looking six months ago. We drive by the property and the lot is not very appealing. It's steep and has a ditch and power lines running down one side. It's also right under the neighborhood bar, which will be quite noisy on weekends, and it faces the motorway. I'm shocked at the price.

We go back to our house and pour over real estate catalogues, translating for our friends. Unlike other countries, there is no multiple listing services. You have to look agent-by-agent, catalog-by-catalog. I can't believe the prices. How can people afford it? Galvin and Barbara are disappointed too. They've bought land in Russia, Hungary and Poland for a tenth of the price. They are willing to pay a little more for Spain but nothing like these prices. They decide to keep the appointments anyway. Perhaps they will get lucky. We walk around our *urbanización* so they can get a feel for the area then back at the house we eat fresh baguettes with tomato and goat cheese.

After lunch, we drive back to *Maçanet* and our first appointment. I listen to Galvin enthusiastically describe his building projects to a young real estate agent who speaks a little English. Galvin tries to explain the kind of property they are interested in and what they want to build. They get on the Internet and Galvin shows off his web pages where there are photos of their various housing projects. Galvin has an ability to make anything sound bigger, better, healthier and more profitable than it really is. He's a born salesman. The agent seems interested but doesn't have a suitable property. They exchange business cards.

The clouds have cleared and the weather has turned hot. Barbara is dying for a swim in the Mediterranean so we go home, grab swimsuits and head to the beach at *Lloret de Mar*. I can't tolerate the water or the sun with my rash so I stay covered from head to toe in a light shirt and pants and sit on the beach and take photos of them swimming. It's early evening and the beach is tranquil. I enjoy watching the people and wonder why we don't take the time to do this more. We hardly ever come to the beach.

We walk the shopping district back to the car warning Galvin and Barbara to watch their pockets. Unfortunately, this is the height of the tourist season and pickpockets are rampant. On the way home we stop at a pizza parlor in *Vidreres* for dinner. Galvin and Barbara are strict vegetarians and Galvin accidentally orders a pizza that has ham on it and has to send it back. The chef replaces it with a vegetarian one for free. We are thankful and leave a good tip. Then we head home to sit on the porch swing and drink wine.

The next morning we drive to *Maçanet*. The weekly market is in session so the main square is full of vendors selling vegetables, meat, cheese, clothing, CD's and plants. The air is filled with the smell of grilled chicken from one of the vendors. I think it smells delicious but Galvin and Barbara are repulsed. The real estate agent is late opening so we buy cherries and sit and eat them outside the agent's office and wait for someone to arrive. Galvin says the cherries are better than anything he can get in England. The agent arrives and Dennis waits in *Maçanet* while the four of us pile into her car to look at the properties. She shows us three properties in an *urbanización* near town. She doesn't speak any English so I act as translator. I find this humorous with my terrible Spanish, but we manage. All the properties are expensive. Galvin is interested in one that is flat, with huge cork oaks scattered around. The land has been cleared so there is a soft layer of pine needle and grass on the ground. I stand with the agent as Galvin and Barbara walk the land. A neighbor comes to chat with the agent and asks what the price is. He shakes his head and walks away when she tells him. I feel like doing the same thing. We look at two more properties that are not as interesting then we head back to town to pick up Dennis.

We show them the land around *LLoret de Mar* and *Blanes*. They are discouraged by the prices. We want to take them to *Tossa de Mar* but Galvin refuses.

"That can't be the name of the town," Galvin tells us. "A British person would die of embarrassment if he had to tell someone he lived in *Tossa*."

"Why?" we ask, we don't understand.

Barbara explains; "It's one of the first slang words I learned when we moved to England. It means masturbate."

On the way home I ask them if they want to visit *Barcelona*. Barbara tells us there is one museum that she would really like to see: the Salvador Dali Museum. I explain to her that it's not in *Barcelona*, but in *Figueras* about sixty kilometers from our house. We offer to take them if they would rather do that than look at more property. Yes, they both agree, they probably can't afford anything in Spain anyway, why not enjoy themselves?

There's a mile long queue at the museum. It's very hot in the sun of the square outside the museum. Every inch of shade is occupied. It's late morning so we decide to eat now then come back to the museum when everyone else goes to lunch. Near the museum, the restaurants are really tourist traps. We can tell by the prices and the billboards lining the sidewalks. Every menu has exactly the same pictures. We finally find a restaurant tucked in a little courtyard that advertises vegetarian *paella*. *Paella* is also on the *menu del dia* so I ask the waiter if they can get vegetarian *paella* instead of the normal version. He checks with the kitchen and says yes. We eat *gazpacho*, the chilled tomato soup that's a summertime Spanish staple. They both like it very much; it's refreshing in the heat of the day. The *paella* arrives and Galvin and Barbara soon discover that that their rice has seafood in it. Galvin turns a pale shade of green. He can't eat a bite. When the waiter returns, I try to explain to the waiter that they don't eat any meat or seafood. He fetches the chef and she comes out waving a spoon in the air and telling me the *paella* is "*sin carne*", without meat. I once again try to explain they can't eat seafood. She finally agrees to exchange it but says they can't have the *menu del dia* price. She pats me on the shoulder and smiles when she leaves. The new *paella* has arrived but about halfway through their meal Galvin discovers a small piece of seafood in his dish. He's horrified. I assume that the chef just didn't bother to change spoons when she filled their plates or she served them normal *paella* with the seafood picked out. Galvin is sick to his stomach and goes to the bathroom to throw up. Barbara keeps eating, she hasn't found any seafood in her rice and it tastes good. Galvin returns and calls the waiter over and points at the tiny bit of crab leg. I know the waiter just doesn't understand. When he picks up the plate behind Galvin's back I see him rolling his eyes. They have a beautiful, wide selection of vegetables here but Spaniards are real meat lovers. Only in *Barcelona* and *Girona* and the most popular tourist cities do they have specialty restaurants catering to vegetarians. Galvin is disgusted and doesn't want to eat anything else. The bill for the lunch is 55 Euro. Expensive considering Galvin couldn't even eat. Dennis and I pay for the meal, we feel bad for what happened. I blame it on my bad Spanish. I just couldn't explain properly. While they wait in the queue at the museum, I go to the supermarket and buy them a bag of *lazos,* a delicious Catalan pastry sprinkled with powdered sugar. They devour the whole bag waiting in the line at the museum.

We drive the back roads to show them more of the country side. The land is dry; we haven't had rain in ages. The trees are still green but the underlying brush is brown and crackled. We explain to Galvin that land is cheaper in the interior of Spain but it will be drier than here, hotter in the summer, colder in the winter. He says he's not interested in anything drier, coming from England this is already too dry for his tastes.

Heading home we see a beautiful blond woman, tall and shapely she is walking down the side of the highway wearing only a thong, a brown net tunic and spiked high heels. She has her back to us and Galvin's mouth falls open as he swings around to get a better look. I explain that she is a prostitute. He can't believe it and wants to us to stop so we can ask her if it's true, he also wants a photo. Luckily, Dennis refuses so Galvin keeps his eyes peeled for the next one. There are more girls down the road but they are dressed in normal street clothes and look like ordinary women waiting for a bus. Galvin is disappointed.

Later that night, we sit drinking wine on the veranda. They loved the Dali Museum. Barbara is an artist and she tells me. "I don't like all his work, but I really respect him as an artist." Suddenly she gets up and runs to the bathroom. She has a bout of diarrhea. "I shouldn't have eaten that *paella,*" she tells me. They have an evening flight home tomorrow night so they decide to spend the next day in *Barcelona.*

Early in the morning I take them to the train station in *San Celoni* and help them buy round trip tickets to the city. I give them a map of *Barcelona* and a train schedule. They promise to be back for dinner. We've had such bad luck eating at restaurants that I plan to make dinner at home; a walnut zucchini pasta. Two hours before their plane leaves they call us from *Barcelona* and say the train is delayed. They are nervous; don't want to miss their flight. Dennis drives to the train station so he is there as soon as they get off the train. They rush home and pack, with only forty-five minutes before their flight they throw things into suitcases and jump in the car. Dennis drops them at the airport and they run for the plane. Dennis waits for a half hour at the airport and they get checked in OK so he comes home. We sit down to eat the cold zucchini pasta and the phone rings. It's Galvin, their flight is delayed for an hour but everything is fine. He says they loved *Barcelona,* spent the whole day in *Casa Batlló.* He tells me, "We really like it here and really want to find a property to buy."

Wildfires, Parasites and Relief

Nearly every night on the news we see raging wildfires. In the southern part of Spain a wildlife refuge is burned and they show graphic photos of charred animal carcasses. There are films of burned earth and scorched firefighters near the eastern coasts of *Valencia*, *Tarragona* and in the northwestern part of the country, *Galicia*. Amateur home owners are fighting together with the professionals to try to save their homes. Most of the residents are forced to abandon their homes and we see pictures of women huddled at the community center, hugging their children and crying. How terrifying it must have been when our little neighborhood here in *Maçanet* experienced a wildfire. No homes were lost though the damage is still visible. All the trees, except the cork oak, are dead and the underbrush is still black with soot. The vegetation is starting to recover, but in the height of this hot, dry summer season the hills around our house are barren and brown in contrast to the lush green of the neighboring hills.

We suffer from the heat, some days the temperatures near 40C. The sun is so bright that is hurts our eyes. I have almost abandoned working in the garden. I have to go out before the sun comes over the nearby mountain top or the sun is so intense that it burns right through my clothes. We leave the shutters rolled down on the windows in our house creating a cool cave like haven inside. The cats spread out on the tile floor, with their fur coats they too are suffering. They leave gobs of fur everywhere and we have to spread towels on the sofa and chairs to keep them clean. Murphy stops eating and stays hidden in the dark back bedroom. When I pick her up she's burning like she's been sitting in a sunny window. She must have a high fever so we rush her to the vet. She's diagnosed with parasites, probably from fighting with another cat or from eating birds and mice. She's given a shot and we buy pills for the next seven days. I worry about her the whole day; she's very sick and can hardly lift her body. The next morning we try to give her one of the pills but they cause her mouth to foam so much that she gags and chokes on her own saliva. I discard the pills and we drive to the vet. I try to explain about the medicine. There's no way I'm going to force these down her throat. The vet agrees with me, "*Yo se*," he tells me, "I know, they aren't good for cats." I wish I knew how to say, "Why the hell do you prescribe them then?" in

Spanish. We have to take Murphy to the vet's office for the next five days for shots. Luckily they only cost a couple of euro a day.

Between the cats and I we seem to throw all our money at doctors and medicine. The vet warns us that the parasites are extremely contagious and it's likely that our other cat will get them. Like a prophesy fulfilled, a month later, Tanya won't eat and has a high fever. This time when the vet tries to prescribe the foam-at-the-mouth-pills, I refuse them. He prescribes a liquid medicine that we can squirt in her mouth instead. After a trip to the pharmacy we find out that this liquid, actually a children's medicine, has exactly the same effect as the pills; enormous foaming at the mouth, choking the cat. I refuse to use it again and we head back to the vet. Why do they prescribe medicine that is impossible to use? I feel so sorry for my little cat and wonder how many times we will have to go through this process. Will my cats just keep passing parasites back and forth? This time the vet gives us bird medicine. We have to give her six pills all at the same time, and repeat the treatment in three weeks. The cat is so sick that I actually manage to give her all six pills, wrapped in butter, without too much struggle. There's one advantage to the cold, north of Norway; less disease, less parasites. It was too cold there even for fleas.

As the seasons change the produce in the restaurants and shops change as well. In late summer we eat figs, peaches, nectarines and watermelon. Peppers are in season and the restaurants are serving them grilled and stuffed with a breaded seafood mixture and a creamy tomato sauce. Delicious! We buy sweet peppers as big as cantaloupe and small deep purple eggplants. The Spanish eat melons like mad, averaging nine kilo per person per summer. They serve it with the salty cured ham and the flavor combination is fantastic. We love to go out to eat but try to keep it to once a week. Our budget and bellies can't take more than that.

In the afternoons, it's too hot to move. Like the cats, Dennis suffers from the heat. He lies on the cool tile floor in front of the fan. He wonders if he has moved to the right place and wishes we had gone to the pines of the Pyrenees Mountains. In the evening when the temperatures cool, we try to sit outside but are chased in by the insects after the sun sets. I itch enough as it is and don't need mosquito bites added to the problem. We buy screens for the windows of the house and leave the windows open all night.

The doctor has changed my medicine once again and asked me to stay on the special diet for six more weeks. I haven't responded to the diet or medicine at all. He tells me if this does not help there is nothing more he can do. "I think this problem could be emotional," he tells me. "How is your life, your husband, your family?" I explain that everything is good, that it's never easy moving to a foreign country but basically it's going well. I like Spain very much and my husband, well he's my best friend. My childhood was good too and I'm close to my parents and siblings. I am one of the lucky ones. I can see in his face that he doesn't believe me; he thinks that I'm hiding a secret abuse or something, but it's true. My only real problem is the rash.

After six more weeks my doctor has thrown his hands in the air. He tells me "I never recommend cortisone but in your case it's all I can do." I'm so discouraged. Cortisone didn't help me before and made my joints swell up. My rash is so painful; it hurts to move my arms, back, shoulders. The heat makes it worse, sweat exacerbates the itching. I have moved to a new level of hell. It makes me wonder if I want to continue. This is no life. Doctors, medicines, time, nothing seems to help me. I see no relief in sight and feel such despair.

Dennis drives me to the medical center in *Girona*. The doctor seems disinterested and spends about three minutes looking at me then recommends a new antihistamine and another cream. I feel hopelessness. What good are yet another antihistamine, yet another cream? I sit in the car and cry. Dennis holds me and rubs my back. He's desperate for me to get better and feels as helpless as I.

At the pharmacy I buy the new antihistamine but debate on whether or not to buy the new cream. It's very expensive, 44 Euro for a small 30 ml tube. The young girl behind the counter looks at my arm then holds up the cream and says, "*es muy bueno, funciona.*" It's really good, it works. She's not a doctor, should I believe her? Dennis tells me to buy it.

The first night with the cream I feel like I am on fire, like there is a fever in my skin. My head is pounding with an intense headache. In a strange way this is a relief for me. I don't sleep the whole night but simply lay there feeling the burning. At least I don't itch.

The next day the burning has lessened. The rash looks red and rough but I continue to use the cream. On the third day my rash looks like it is beginning to heal. I begin to feel hope but am scared I will be disappointed once again. After the first week I'm definitely better. I still have periods of intense itching, but they are becoming fewer and fewer. I look at my red hamburger skin and wonder if it can really heal. I can sleep for a few hours every night now. Relief washes through my body. I'm so grateful to not itch-like I have been given a new life.

You Don't Need Papers for a Garage

One Saturday morning in late September Pedro's wife Luisa waves hello to me from across the street. I harvest four leeks from my garden, clip the roots and wash them off and walk across the street to give them to her. She has given me green beans, eggplant and zucchini from her garden. I am glad to finally be able to give her something in return. She invites me to look at her house and garden. Another neighbor, Maria, from up the street is visiting and they show me around the small house and big garden. They both talk the whole time and I try to keep up, with difficulty. Luisa apologizes for the small house but I say, "*Vår hus es mas pequeno.*" Our house is smaller. Then realize I have spoken to her in a combination of Norwegian and Spanish. Her house is older than ours and she explains that she and her husband Pedro have been coming here every weekend for twenty-four years. Maria says "*nosotros tambien*" that she and her husband have done the same thing. It's hard to believe so I shake my head and say "*incredible*".

Pedro is the gardener in the family. He is outside watering as I take my tour. He comes and greets me with a big smile. His garden is huge with at least thirty bean plants, thirty tomatoes and row after row of eggplant, chard, spring onions, spinach. I'm really impressed and tell him the garden is "*bonito*", beautiful. He tells me that they had *estiercol* brought in on big trucks. I should do the same thing and then my garden will be better too. They load me up with chard, egg-plant and a strange prickly fruit plucked from a vine, explaining I should eat it fresh in salad.

I head toward the gate and try to wave good bye with my arms full. Maria walks with me and explains that her husband helped to build our house. He is a cousin of the old owner. I invite her to come and see the house and take a pump-kin from the garden. She walks inside, greets Dennis and tells us that the house was once a garage. "*No necesita papeles por un garaje.*" You don't need papers for a garage. She continues to paint a history of our little house. First, it was a garage then a room was added for the bathroom. A wall was inserted to separate the kitchen then two rooms added at the back for bedrooms. Slowly, the garage became a house and the authorities had no idea. Then after all the work and all the years, the man becomes sick and has to sell.

I tell the story to Marta later and she nods her head in agreement. "It's the way things are done here," she says. "These people they come from *Andalucía*, from small villages in the country. There is nothing there, no work, no money and so they come to *Barcelona* and get jobs. Maybe they work in a little shop or factory somewhere and live in a high rise apartment. They live in a tiny room and have no green around them and they miss it desperately. Their dream is to have a house in the country so they save every *centimo* until they can buy land. Then they eventually put up a garage. You don't need papers to build a garage. There is no way they can afford an architect or a builder so they come every weekend and build a little at a time until one day they have a house." Suddenly the "illegalness" of our house takes on a meaning that wasn't there before and my frustration is transformed into admiration for these clever hard working people.

Lunch with Italians

It's time for Spanish classes to start again. At registration we greet the teacher and fellow students like old friends. Many students from our first class are continuing this year. Perhaps it's because we have a little more Spanish or maybe we just feel more comfortable with each other but the conversations are warm and lively. Natalia apologizes for not calling; she was away most of the summer. The Italians are there too and after greeting us with a kiss on each cheek, they invite us to their home for lunch the following Sunday.

Our Spanish teacher is quite obviously pregnant. Dennis makes a comment to her, "*Tu tienes un poco mas peso, ahora*", you have a little more weight, now. She smiles and pats her belly. "*Si, yo estoy comiendo para dos.*" Yes, I'm eating for two. Dennis pats his belly and says, "*yo tambien.*" Me, too. The teacher does not understand this is a joke. She exclaims, "*no, no, no, no, no, no, no. Tu no estas comiendo pare dos, es imposible!*" You are not eating for two, its impossible! Dennis just laughs and says, but look at me I am! Then she understands and laughs too.

Lunch at Marianna and Enrico's house is lovely. They live in an *urbanización* near the house we rented from Marta. We greet them and almost immediately sit down to lunch. We agree at the outset that we will try to use Spanish as much as possible. Like us, they have little contact with the locals and need the practice. Marianna has made a pâté with toasted bread for an appetizer. She tells us to go ahead and eat. She will start cooking the pasta. "You can't cook pasta ahead of time, you have to do it right before you eat or it's ruined." She makes a beautiful pesto Genovese, the basil is from their garden and the pine nuts were collected in the wild. Enrico tells us they walk in the woods nearly everyday collecting pine nuts, wild mushrooms, asparagus or blackberries, depending on the season. Marianna says that she loves it here, loves the life style. Enrico doesn't however. "If I had known about all the bureaucracy, I would never have come. I even had to take a driving test. I've been driving for forty years. I had a license from South Africa and one from America but they wouldn't accept either of those." He waves his arms as he talks, speaking in a blend of Italian, Spanish and English, "I don't like the people here either. They are like Italians in the south, they are not honest, and you cannot trust them." We ask if they've had a bad experience. "Well, yes and no. We added a bedroom onto the house. It was OK for two of us, but when our son came to visit it was a bit small. We were thinking of adding as bedroom and told a friend of ours. One day he shows up with a crew of men. We had no agreement but I felt bad saying no so we let him do the work. He was a friend of mine. He's not one now. He did a very bad job. I had to fix everything."

Marianna watches me eat the long strings of pasta and corrects me. "You are taking too much on your fork. It makes it difficult. Only take a small amount and twist it around." I try a sample bite and she tells me, "Still too much, smaller." I find out she's right. How could I have missed something so obvious all these years? After the pasta Marianna serves marinated slices of beef with some steamed vegetables. She's an excellent cook.

The meal has made me warm so I remove a light sweater I am wearing and Enrico immediately grabs my arm and points to the rash remaining on my elbows. "What's this?" he exclaims. I try to explain about the rash, that the doctors think it is an allergy but he interrupts me. "I have the same thing," he says. He brushes his fingers through his wavy gray hair. "On my head, I have these little spots that itch like crazy."

I'm amazed at how many people I meet now who have problems with eczema. Since it is difficult for me to hide it, nearly everyone I meet tells me they have a problem with it or knows someone who does. Two of my neighbors have asked me about the rash on my arms. When I explained about my allergies one told me her little granddaughter has the same thing. "It's the sun. She can't tolerate it." The other tells me her son has the same thing. "It's olives, he can't eat olives." Is this the epidemic of our time? How many people have a rash hidden under their clothes, spending sleepless nights scratching?

After lunch we sit in the living room and chat. They tell us stories about living in America and South Africa. They both loved living in America. They lived in a small town in Indiana and thought the people were very nice although they tell me they never met a single person who was "*delgada*" thin, like me. "We saw thin people on TV but never in real life. Everyone we met was very fat."

Their favorite place was South Africa. They lived there for twenty years and didn't want to leave. Marianna explains, "It got so bad in the end we just couldn't stay. We had to put electric gates around all the houses to be safe. One of our friends drove her car home one day and was stopped at her gate when a bunch of men tried to steal her car. She threw the car keys over the gate so they couldn't steal it. They got so mad at her that they beat her up. All the men had to carry guns to protect themselves. Enrico wore one everywhere he went. Some other friends of ours had family come visit. They rented a big van so they could go on a tour of a wildlife preserve and they were loading it up with food one morning and had their gate open. A group of men came and tried to steal the van. Our friend put his hand on his hip as an instinct, reaching for his gun, and they shot him. He was killed right there with his whole family watching. It had been so nice to live there before we didn't want to leave. In the end it was our son who left. His best friend at school was murdered and he just couldn't stay there. He decided to go to university in England. We just couldn't live that way any longer and with our son gone we decided to leave too."

Later they give us a tour of the house and garden. They have a cistern like we do and use it all summer but now it is empty. Enrico complains about the cost of water. "Those are very expensive vegetables, next year I will let them die rather than pay for the water." Suddenly Marianna has a pain in her foot. She's wearing a sundress with sandals and I can see that her foot is bright red. I wonder if it is a bite but she says no, it's something internal. As we say our goodbyes she limps to the car. What in the world is wrong?

At Spanish class the next day Marianna is still limping. She tells us that her foot is much better now but the evening before it really swelled up and was very painful. She has no idea what it could be but now it's getting better she will probably never know.

Booty Ferry

The Spanish amaze me in the way they treat animals. They either love them madly or treat them like dirt. There doesn't seem to be much in between. Waiting at the vet's office the pet owners always chat about their animals and ask after ours. They want to know their names, how old they are and what's the matter? The vet's are very gentle and caring. One vet told me he has sixteen cats, another has eleven. In contrast, we see abandoned dogs and cats everywhere, especially at the trash bins. Half of the people in our *urbanización* abandon their animals and the other half carry bags of food out to the dump every night to feed them.

Marta tells us Spanish people laugh if you tell them you paid money to get a cat or dog sterilized. The concept is completely foreign to them. There are no government initiatives to control the situation, no education. What a contrast to Norway. When we first moved there we were told that it was illegal to sterilize your animal because it was an infringement on the animal's rights. Even the cows in Norway have to be given a certain number of days outside every year; they're entitled to a holiday too.

One day we stop at the recycling center at the entrance to our *urbanización* as we head out to the coast. I throw the metal and plastic into their separate bins then move to the bins for glass and bottles. Stunned, I see there are three small puppies in a cardboard box next to the bin. It's early on a Sunday morning and they yip and jump when they see me. Too small to climb out of the box they tumble over each other. I can't believe someone has just left them here. I don't know what to do. Back at the car I tell Dennis about them.

He says, "That's too bad" then gets in the car to leave.

I get angry. "We can't just leave them! They're just tiny puppies!"

Dennis tells me, "We have two cats and with your allergies, we can't have any dogs. You know that."

I know he's right but I can't just leave them. Maybe we should talk to the vet and see what he recommends but it's Sunday and the vet is closed. There's a phone number in the vet's office for abandoned animals. Maybe we can call someone? But, no, because it's Sunday and we can't get to it. There's supposed to be a dog shelter near *Tossa de Mar*. We don't know where it is. We don't know its name and don't have a phone book.

Dennis says, "Let's just leave. We can't even talk properly. Leave it to a Spanish person."

I don't know. "What if no one comes? They can't stay in that box all day and night with no food or water."

"Ok," he says, "I'll make you a deal. When we come home in a few hours, if they're still there, they can stay at the house overnight. But you have to get rid of them on Monday." I agree, but when we return a few hours later the box and puppies are gone.

It's time for our cat's yearly rabies shots so we haul them in their cages back to the vet in *Maçanet*. He recognizes us immediately and says in a mixture of English and Spanish, "How is the *caca*?" Have I heard correctly? *How is the shit?* Then I realize he's asking about the cat's parasites. "*Muy bien,*" we say, very good. Then I realize that was a stupid answer. Their excrement is very good? But he seemed to understand that everything is OK.

Our cat, Tanya, was the runt of the litter. She's so tiny and thin that a stranger seeing her on the street would think she was starving. She's healthy though and has a sporadic but good appetite so we don't worry about her. Murphy, on the other hand, lives to eat and has a figure to show it. As the vet removes Tanya from her cage he says, "*Venga guapa.*" Come here, pretty. After giving Tanya her shots he tries to remove Murphy from her cage. She doesn't want to come out. He says, "*Venga, gordita.*" Come here, little fatty. I'm so embarrassed. I apologize. "*Lo siento,*" I say, "I'm sorry, she loves to eat. I have a hard time refusing her."

He tells us, "I had an English couple in here last week. They had a very fat dog. They told me he looked like a Booty Ferry. 'I don't know this word,' I told them. They try to explain; 'You know a Booty Ferry, like the Catalan sausage.' No, I don't know this word. Then a light goes off in my head. They try to say the Catalan word *botifarra*. It's true the dog has on a little sweater and he looks just like one."

We all start laughing.

A Year in Spain

We have been in Spain almost a year. The autumn has arrived and we look forward to the cooler weather. We've begun our second semester of Spanish classes and we have started to meet for coffee with the other students after class. The teacher remembers our names and greets us with a big smile. The tourists are leaving and *Lloret* is returning to a quiet beach town.

The rain has started and the land is turning green once again. With my rash slowly disappearing and the itching eased, I am feeling well enough to go for walks with Dennis. The land around our house is still scarred from the wildfire. The cork oaks are thriving; immigrants still scour the countryside collecting bark. I'm amazed that even with the bark gone, the trees survived the wildfire. The undergrowth is starting to return, mostly the noxious wild blackberry. There are birds singing everywhere. In the evenings we can hear frogs croaking in the creek below our house. I love this time of year with warm sunny days and cool nights.

We've started to spend more time in the nearby town of *Maçanet*. It's a very ordinary pueblo but I find it absolutely charming. The town is a mix of old and new. An old stone church sits in the center of the town plaza surrounded by little stone shops, modern glass fronted banks and concrete apartment blocks. The town has everything; a post office, a vet, a swimming pool, a church and a city square, a bookstore and newspaper stand, a dentist and a barber. It has three banks, three grocery stores, three clothing shops. I try to explain to Carlos why I like it. When I tell him it has six bakeries and six bars he smiles with admiration, "Six bars!" That sounds good." On summer evenings they show old films in a small outdoor plaza. On Sunday mornings there's a van parked in the city square where they sell *churros con chocolate*. Every Wednesday morning there's a street market. The people of the pueblo are starting to recognize us. We have learned to say *buenas* when we enter a shop or bakery and remember to say *hasta luego* when we leave. Spanish people don't form lines while waiting. When we enter a shop, we've learned to ask, "*quien is la ultima?*" Who is last? Then we watch for that person to be served because we will be next.

Our Spanish is slowly improving. I made an appointment at the dentist today and mailed a package to America. Two activities that were daunting a year ago now don't seem so difficult. We no longer panic when the phone rings, worried we won't understand. Slowly, slowly we are feeling more comfortable. Slowly, slowly we are adapting to this pace of life. Slowly, slowly we are feeling that this is home.

TV and War

Our house sits in a valley and the only TV channels we get are two Catalan stations. I know I will have to learn some Catalan eventually but, for now, my head is full of Spanish. I'm not ready to take on another language.

We want to listen to more Spanish, to practice the language and know what is going on around us. These were our excuses for buying a satellite dish and receiver. Unfortunately this has backfired on us. We do watch the Spanish stations, but with four free news channels in English we end up watching these most of the time.

I'm so depressed by the war in Iraq. Almost every day we see the body bags and coffins of US soldiers. I've heard they've banned the American TV channels from showing photos of the coffins. Today the Madrid news station showed a close up of three coffins draped in USA flags then, the camera panned backward revealing not three, but tens, then hundreds, of flag draped coffins. Why shouldn't the American people see this? The dead are their children, husbands and brothers and this is the reality of war.

The Spanish news is incredibly graphic. We see the dead bodies of Iraqi men and women. We see Iraqi mothers wailing over the bodies of their dead children. We see massive pools of blood on the streets. I'm overwhelmed, horrified. The US forces haven't found a single weapon of mass destruction, the reason the government gave for invading that country. Another day on the news we see that ammunitions silos in Iraq have been looted. Before the war, this site was inventoried and placed under UN weapons inspector lock and key. Now it's been looted. They say no one was guarding the silo. No one knows who has those weapons now. They say that not a single weapon silo has been guarded during this war; in fact the only government building that has been guarded is the ministry of oil. How can this be? I hear a speech by President Bush and he says the world is safer now than it was before the war was started. Which world does he live in? The news might be filtered for the American people but it certainly can't be filtered for him. Or can it?

I've been using the eczema cream for about three months. I've stopped seeing the homeopathic doctor. I'm using one tube of medicine a week and at 45 Euro a pop, I simply can't afford the eczema medicine and the doctor visits. The rash is 80% healed but the last bit is stuck; it just refuses to go away. I feel better, I mean I don't itch like I used to. Well, I still itch but it's at such a low level compared to what it was before that I feel like I've got my life back. On the other hand, I have little energy and my allergies are terrible. I hoped that, with the onset of autumn and winter, they would disappear but they've actually worsened. I don't know if I have constant colds or if I have allergies. I've been sick continuously for the last three months. As soon as I recover from one cold, I come down with another. My homeopathic doctor told me if your mucus has color it's a cold, if it's clear; it's an allergy. I was so surprised when he told me this. How can I be almost fifty years old and not know this? Anyway, yellow snot or not, the roof of my mouth itches all the time so I think it's allergies. My asthma is worse too. I can't go on walks with Dennis unless I take my inhaler. The hills just do me in. I am concerned about using this eczema cream for so long. The instructions say that I should only use the medicine for a month but when I stop the rash and itching return.

Two weeks ago I came down with influenza big time. I was bed ridden with fever and body aches for three days. I was so congested that I had to sleep sitting up. I didn't even want to get up to pee. Dennis drove me to the clinic in *Girona*. I was so dizzy he had to help me walk across the street. Now the fever has broken and my chest is clearing but I still have a cough that shakes my whole body. My stomach muscles are still sore from coughing.

Dennis and I rack our brains trying to figure out what is causing my health problems. With every flare up we discuss what I ate, drank, and which clothes I have worn. What soap did I use? Where did I go? Were the cats in the house or out? Did we use the fireplace? Where did we walk? There are hundred of possibilities and countless combinations, we are stumped. There's no consistent pattern. I wear nothing but white cotton; use no make up, avoid anything with perfume and use the barest dabs of soap. We've bought a new mattress for the bed and dust mite covers for the mattress and pillows. We wash all the linens in hot water and we've bought an air purifier. I've tried eliminating all but the most basic foods from my diet. I've given up caffeine and alcohol. I drink only purified water. I wear a face mask in the garden. Nothing helps.

Back at Spanish class Marianna tells me she too has had this influenza and it was terrible. I have trouble concentrating in class which is too bad; we are finally learning the past tense of some verbs. We've been here over a year and I will finally be able to say something in the past tense. Unfortunately the teacher informs us that this form of the past tense is not used very much. It's only used to talk about something with an indefinite time period. There's another form for talking about yesterday or last week. Great. Why do they teach us the version we are NOT supposed to use first? We get a homework assignment to write a short paragraph about our childhood. The paragraph starts; *Cuando yo era nina*…When I was a child…

I write a story about going to my grandmother's house with my brother and sister. She had a big closet full of games. My sister and I could spend hours playing with a jar of buttons. She also had sweets, like Ding Dongs and Twinkies, which our mother never bought. My essay makes me homesick for my family.

Dennis writes about growing up and not having any friends, about loving to read and sneaking a flashlight under the bed covers to secretly read at night. I don't think he feels the same homesickness I do.

We are asked to read our essays out loud in class. Enrico doesn't want to read his. He says it was about war, the Americans bombing his house in Italy, about how his grandmother made him hide under a table when the bombs were dropping. After class he grabs my arm, "I don't hate Americans," he shrugs his shoulders and turns his palms up. "War is war."

I'm so curious about the medicine I'm using. I dig one of the information sheets out of the trash. Of course I've read it before but now I want the dirty details. I have to sit with a Spanish dictionary to read it. I'm wondering if congestion and asthma could be a side affect from the medicine. Curiously some of the side effects are rashes, itching and burning; the very thing it's trying to cure. It says nothing about asthma or congestion but it does say that I shouldn't take a vaccination while I'm using the medicine or for at least thirty days after I stop. I wonder why. I decide to look up the active ingredient *tacrolimus* on the Internet. I find out it's an immune suppressant. It was first developed for organ transplant patients to help prevent their immune systems from rejecting new organs. Later, it was made into a topical cream for eczema treatment. Whoa! I have read that allergies and eczema are the result of an over active immune system. Your body is reacting to something that most people can tolerate. In a way it makes sense but this is serious stuff. I suspect the medicine is one reason I keep getting sick. With a suppressed immune system I have no resistance to any virus that happens along.

Homesick Christmas

We don't put up a Christmas tree this year. The house is so small we really don't know where to put it. Instead, we hang some tinsel in the window and dangle some crystal ornaments from it. The crystals throw prisms on the wall when the sun shines during the day and it's beautiful.

I want to cook a turkey for Christmas dinner. It's been ages since we've had one and now I finally have an oven. The only whole birds I find are two poor fellows where the packages have been ripped open and the meat is dried. I settle for two turkey legs. I make dressing and mash potatoes and from a family recipe; wonderful, garlic breadsticks. The breadsticks have to be started the day before and left to rise in the fridge overnight. Happy memories of Christmas with my family come barreling at me as I smell them cooking. I feel so homesick I'm going to bust. Christmas is the most depressing time for me. After all these years away from my parents, my brother and sister, I should be used to it but I'm not. I love living in Europe but I really hate being so far away from my family.

One year my parents came to Norway for Christmas. My mother wanted to experience the Norwegian winter just once. We took them to a mountain hotel for a Christmas Eve buffet. The Norwegians really know how to lay a buffet; turkey and chicken and all kinds of vegetables, salads, and soups and breads. There was the traditional Christmas fare of *ribbe*, spareribs; *pinnekjøtt*, steamed and roasted mutton and about fifteen kinds of fish. Our Norwegian friends insisted that we try the ultra traditional *lutefisk*. The dictionary says that this is, "cod, treated in a lye solution and served boiled." Perhaps it is best described as fish jello. There was *råkefisk*, trout that has been buried until it ferments. Both these delicacies taste terrible. Maybe they are acquired tastes and you have to start young? I had to spit the *råkefisk* into my napkin. Christmas day brought a snow storm followed by a deep freeze. My parents got to see ice crystals freezing into layers and layers on the pine trees. They were awed by fields of huge ice crystals sparkling like jewels in the mild midday sun. On New Years Eve the temperature dropped to -20C. When we stood outside at midnight to drink champagne and watch the fireworks, the glasses stuck to our lips. What a contrast to Three Kings day at the beach! All these memories come pouring back to me as Dennis and I sit alone at home on Christmas Eve.

South to Tarragona

Marta is convinced that it is our house that is causing my allergies. Dennis thinks it might be the environment around the house; perhaps the cork oak or residue from the wild fire? There are industries in the area and we wonder if the air pollution is irritating me. I decide to make a trip to America, to see if my health improves. We decide I should stay away at least a month, in a month a body can replace its skin cells.

I return from America feeling better. My sinuses have cleared; no more itchy mouth and runny eyes and no more asthma attacks. Two days after returning to Spain I'm sick again. I'm congested, coughing and my asthma is so bad I can't even carry a bag of groceries without wheezing. Marta tells me the problem could be our cats. I can't believe it's the cats because I don't feel worse when I cuddle them. If I get near a horse or cow I get instant asthma but Murphy can come and sit on my lap and get petted and I feel no different. Besides my sister had two cats and I was OK at her house. Dennis and I discuss moving. How can I continue to live in a place where I'm not healthy?

We can't afford to live on the coast which would probably be the healthiest. We decide to make a trip inland to *Huesca* where it's drier than *Catalunya*. Then we will head north to the mountains of the Pyrenees, where we hope there is little industry. We do the trip in two days so we don't have to put the cats in a kennel. We drive first to the small city of *Monson* in the region of *Huesca* just west across the border of *Catalunya*. There's an interesting fortress on the hill overlooking the town but the surrounding country is flat dry desert. The town looks run down, dejected. We find the area depressing.

The countryside becomes more interesting as we head north. The land becomes mountainous and although still quite dry, there are lakes and vegetation. We can see the snow capped mountains in the distance. After living in Norway for so long we long for the mountains. Skipping all the small towns on the *mesa* we head straight for the snow and pine trees. The country side is so beautiful, the mountains jagged and covered with pines and rock. There are few *pueblos* mostly tiny ski resorts. Typically for Spain, we see few houses with yards. The *pueblos* have apartment blocks then nothing but wilderness at the edge of town with an occasional *masia*. We stop and look in the real estate windows and are shocked at the prices. These are as high as anything on the coast. We would like to rent for a year and ask at a few agents if they have any rentals. Nothing with gardens, nothing for cats, nothing long term. Heading west, farther into the mountains we find the same thing. We stop at small villages and ask at the *ayuntamiento* to see if there are any village houses to rent. Nothing. Nowhere.

We make a trip to the county of *Tarragona*, farther south in *Catalunya*. The climate is dry here, with olive and citrus groves instead of cork oak. The land is bone dry and bare beneath the trees and most of it is terraced with stone walls. The city of *Tarragona* is charming but polluted. It's also expensive. We head south and follow the coast for about an hour then turn inland, heading west into the mountains. The country is beautiful here too, but drier than the north. The mountains are covered with pine, but they are scrub pine, not the tall soaring trees of the Pyrenees. We stop and have lunch at the charming *pueblo* of *Tvissa*. It sits half way up a mountain ridge, surrounded by orchards of plum, and peach. We sit in a plaza under the shade of a tree and eat our picnic lunch. A group of old men are sitting on a bench next to us chatting. I try to listen but they are speaking Catalan and I don't understand a word. I look around at the mountains towering behind the village and down the hill at the orchards and think we could live here.

I've been searching the Internet for a house to rent in the province of *Tarragona*. There are tons of stuff for rent by the week but nothing long term. The weekly prices are equal to our monthly budget so I keep searching and searching. Finally, I stumble across a Spanish page advertising rentals and find a house near the coast for rent for 500 Euro a month. I sit for a few minutes practicing what I will say then dial the phone number. I struggle on the telephone asking about the house when the woman suddenly switches to English. I'm so relieved. We make an appointment to meet tomorrow at noon in the small town of *L'Ampollla*, about an hour south of the city of *Tarragona*. She assures me the drive will only take two hours from *Girona* but we know it is closer to three. Our little Peugeot can't manage more than 110 kph so we don't fly like the Spanish.

The town of *L'Ampolla* is small with shiny new buildings lining the waterfront marina. We find a place to park and walk up and down the marina, looking at the boats until noon approaches. Then I make a call.

We are told to come to the *Roca Grossa Hotel* right on the waterfront. We turn and look at the buildings and we are standing nearly in front of it. A man and woman walk out the doors and greet us then wave for us to follow them inside. We sit at the back of the cafe where they are finishing breakfast. We order coffee.

Frieda is very attractive. She is tall and thin with blond, shoulder length hair. She's impeccably dressed and I feel sloppy in my sweat shirt and jeans. She introduces us to her husband Alejandro. I explain that we have a house in *Girona* but we want to move to *Tarragona* for my health. She points to Alejandro and says that he is a doctor. She turns to him and translates what I've said to Spanish. She asks him if a drier climate will help my asthma. He nods and says, "*Si*, sometimes, yes."

She warns us that the house they are renting is very basic, not fancy. They insist on paying for our coffees and we get in our separate cars and follow them to the house. As we head inland from *L'Ampolla* the road turns into a gravel cow path and we wind through olive and orange groves. There are *finca's* dotted here and there and finally we pull into a gated property. Alejandro unlocks the tall, iron gates and waves us through. The long driveway is lined with oleander about shoulder height. The house sits back from the road about a hundred meters. The day is cloudy and overcast and the dirt is damp from a light rain. Frieda tells me that this weather makes her depressed. She doesn't feel right unless it's sunny.

The house sits in the middle of an olive orchard. It has a long sloped roof and looks new. Inside there are terracotta tiles on the floor and light yellow plaster walls. The house smells of mold but it quickly disappears as Frieda rolls up the shutters and opens the windows. The bottom floor is one large room, divided in half by a set of free standing closets. There's a staircase on one wall leading to an upstairs bedroom. I puzzle that there is no kitchen but when I ask about it Frieda raises her hand and tells me, "wait; you will see."

We walk outside, around to the back of the house and there is another tiny stone house attached to the back. It's obviously quite old. She explains that this was the original house. There's a big iron gate across the door and the house is cold, dark and musty when we enter. Here too she rolls up the shutters and opens the windows. Now I see a tiny rustic kitchen, just four burners and a ceramic counter, no oven. The walls are crumbly plaster and there are shelves from about 1950 on one wall. Frieda walks to a large cupboard in the middle of the kitchen, opens the doors and pulls down a bed. It's a wall bed! These things really exist. I feel like I have stepped into a bizarre *I Love Lucy* episode. On one end of the kitchen there is a loft with a tiny staircase and bed. Under the loft is a storage area and next to it a small bathroom. This could be a tiny apartment in its own right but a depressing one. My mind is whirring. What would it be like to have to walk outside to the back of the house every time we want to use the kitchen or go to the fridge? There's a small stone patio outside the kitchen and in the summer we could eat there but what about the winter? There's no room for a table in this kitchen. In the backyard there is a BBQ and an old stone oven. Alejandro walks me over to the oven and explains that it was for making bread and pizza. I get excited thinking of making a pizza in this old traditional way. Where could I get my hands on one of those long flat pizza shovels?

Opposite the BBQ there's a large concrete pond, about 10 feet by 5 feet and about 4 feet deep. As we walk toward it we hear Plop! Plop! Frogs are jumping into the water. Below the pond the land slopes down toward a ravine and Alejandro tells me it's the place for a *huerto*, a kitchen garden, and you can use the pond to water it. It's knee high in weeds but he tells me the soil is ready for planting. I get so excited just thinking about it. I love gardening and could probably grow all year round here.

Alejandro shows Dennis the cistern beneath the house that holds water for drinking, laundry and showers. He tells us the water comes from a community well, he will show us later. Its good water, the well is deep; he tells us but don't drink it. The neighbors drink it but we don't. Frieda explains to me that there are many houses here in the country but there are two big problems in this area; water and electricity. They tell us there should be a new electric line connected to the house soon, that right now we share the neighbor's line. "The electric company says it will be installed in two weeks, but this is Spain so it will be at least a month." I think to myself at least two months but don't say it aloud.

We walk the property and it's huge, about 20,000 square meters of olive and almond trees. The house sits low in a valley with terraced olive trees on the surrounding hills. Alejandro explains that there is too much wind on the hilltops; it's better to be in the valley. Several thousand meters from the house and two terraces up, there is a view of the Mediterranean and someone has installed a BBQ and picnic table at this spot. What a long way to carry your food and drinks!

Dennis and I lag behind as we walk the rest of the land, making a loop back to the house. Dennis says it would be fine for him and we really need to do something to improve my health. The climate is exactly what we were looking for and there's no pollution or industry anywhere near. He thinks we should take it, but he will leave it up to me. I ask Alejandro if they spray the olive trees. He tells me only twice a year, once for insects when the fruit is almost ripe and once when the trees flower in May. There's a *Señor* who cares for the orchard and if we rent it we will meet him. I'm reluctant about the kitchen setup but it seems a small price to pay for better health. I'm so tired of being sick. I'm using an inhaler all the time for asthma. I've had chronic bronchitis for six months and pollen season is starting soon in *Girona*.

I ask Frieda if they would be able to remove some of the furniture if we moved in, we have our own mattress with a cover for dust mites and the curtains will have to go. She says it's no problem; they have another small house just across the road where they can store things. In fact we would be neighbors.

I can see that Frieda and Alejandro love this place. Alejandro runs energetically around showing Dennis the irrigation system. Frieda tells me that she planted all the plants here one by one. The whole house is surrounded by ice plant and I can't imagine all that work. Dennis presses me to make a decision. No use waiting and then having to make the three hour drive again just to sign papers when we could do everything right now. I look at the rash on my arm then over at the pond and imagine a garden filled with peppers and corn and pumpkin and make a decision. One year it is.

Robbed

Tomorrow we are moving to Tarragona. I'm sad to move. I won't miss our little house much but I will miss Marta and Carlos and our neighbors Pedro, Luisa and Maria. I will miss Marianna, Enrico and our fellow students at Spanish class. I will miss our Spanish professor. We were just beginning to know people, to have a social life and now, once again, we will be starting all over.

I wake up shaken in the middle of the night from a nightmare. I've dreamed that the house we've rented doesn't have a kitchen sink. I lay awake in bed and try to remember if I saw a kitchen sink. I simply can't remember and have a panic attack. How can we live without a kitchen sink?

I wake Dennis up and ask him, "Does the house have a kitchen sink?"

"What?" It takes him a minute to wake up. "Of course it does."

"No, I know it should have one but do you actually REMEMBER seeing one because I don't."

He rolls over unconcerned. "It has a kitchen sink."

If this were Norway or America I would just ignore this anxiety attack but this is Spain. There is a strong likelihood that the house has no sink. "Promise me," I ask him. "If it doesn't have one, you'll put one in won't you? I mean even if we are only renting and you'll put one in? I can't live for a year without a kitchen sink."

"Yes, I'll put one in," he says. "Go to sleep."

We've packed up the cats and a few necessities and moved down to Tarragona. I'm so tired of being sick that we don't want to delay it any longer. My dependency on the inhaler is increasing everyday. I can't even walk from the house to the car without an asthma attack. I feel like I'm caught in a terrible cycle of sickness. If I stop using the eczema cream my bronchitis starts to clear but I start to itch. If I use the cream I get asthma and bronchitis. Hopefully this move will help me break the cycle.

The day we arrive I'm relieved to see there's a sink in the kitchen. I wipe out the cupboards and throw away old food and papers Frieda and Alejandro have left. There's a mildew smell in the house so we roll up all the rugs and remove the linens and open all the windows to air it. The cats explore every corner of the house and soon want outside. After three moves in such a short time I'm confident they won't run away so I let them out.

For some reason we've started calling the old stone house the *little house* and the new part the *big house*. If I want to make a cup of tea I tell Dennis I am going, not to the kitchen but, to the little house. The weather is still chilly and the wind has started to blow. There are enormous high voltage power lines behind the house that whine in the wind like a Banshee. We roll down the shades on the windows and turn on the electric floor heaters we brought from Norway. With the vaulted ceiling we can't seem to get the house warm. I feel depressed sitting here listening to the wind. God what have we done?

The wind howls all night and we don't sleep. The cats must be cold because they cuddle on the bed between us. For both of them to be together is unusual. They have their own rules about sharing and usually don't sleep on the bed or even in the same room at the same time. I have to get up in the middle of the night to put an extra comforter on the bed. How will we be able to live in this house all winter? It's April and it's freezing. First thing in the morning we'll have to buy some firewood.

The next day we drive to *L'Ampolla* and stop at the *ayuntamiento* to ask where we can buy firewood. They look at me like I'm crazy, why ask here? We don't know where to go so we drive toward *Tortosa*, the biggest city around. We stop at every petrol station and garden shop we see. In *Girona* this is where they sold wood, but here there is nothing. We drive through *Tortosa*. It's Sunday and everything is closed. Finally we see a house advertising oranges for sale. There's a big stack of wood next to the driveway so, on an off chance, we stop.

There are two old men standing outside chatting and I ask, "*Vende usted leña?*" Do you sell firewood?

He shakes his head. No—oranges, not firewood.

I say OK and turn to leave. His friend stops me and asks, "*Necesita mucho?*" Do you need much?

"*No, no, solo para unos pocos dias,*" only for a couple of days. "*El coche es pequeño tambien.*" The car is small too.

He shakes his head again. No. No wood. Do you want some oranges?

No. I say, just firewood. I get in the car to leave but I see them waving their hands. I tell Dennis, "Stop!"

I roll down the window and the old man tells me: I will sell you some wood, not much, but some.

"*Muchas gracias!*" I jump out of the car before he changes his mind.

We form a human chain. At one end the old man has climbed on top of the wood pile and is handing the wood down to his friend, his friend to me and me to Dennis who loads the trunk. One man is talking the whole time explaining; this wood is for his family, for the winter. It's good, dry wood.

I keep thanking him and explain that we are renting a house that is very cold.

After a couple of armloads the trunk is full. The old man tells me 10 Euro. It's an outrageously high price for what we got but we don't argue. I hand over the money and the old man's friend tells me, "*Es en buen precio, hasta quince euros es bueno.*" It's a good price, maybe even 15 Euro is a good price. The old man shakes his head like even he can't believe that lie. We get in the car to leave and he taps my window. Do you want some oranges?

"*No*, I tell him, "*pero gracias por la leña,*" but thanks for the wood.

Tomorrow I will call Frieda and ask her where to buy wood.

The first time I try to use the washing machine in the little house the electricity goes out. Dennis has to walk up to the neighbors to flip the breaker, but it does no good. Every time we turn on the washer it cuts out again. I call Frieda to explain the problem. We don't have a phone line at the house so we have to rely on our mobile phones. The reception is so bad that she can't understand me so I have to walk up on the hill behind the house to talk to her. Even then, the quality is so bad that we agree to communicate with text messages instead of voice. I send her a message and explain about the washer. She promises to call an electrician and he shows up the next day. When he tries the washer, it works fine. We try different settings but everything is fine. As soon as he leaves, however the electricity goes out again. Such bad luck, but typical. I have to go up on the hill to call him to come back. After a week and three visits from the electrician, he can't find a problem and we can't wash clothes. Frieda is very concerned; she says she needs to wash nearly everyday. How can I wait a week? She decides to buy a new washer and has it delivered immediately. I'm so grateful for her help and the new washer works fine. I think we've been so lucky with landlords since we moved to Spain. First Marta was terrific and now Frieda seems to be too.

The next week the wind is still blowing like the devil. Dennis has hung a clothesline in a dead olive tree but we can't hang clothes out to dry because they are blown off the line. We wonder if this wind is seasonal or if it blows like this constantly. We can see huge wind turbines on the mountains in the distance. Obviously, this is a windy area if they can keep those huge turbines moving. Once again and not for the last time, we wonder if we have made a mistake.

Frieda explains that we should not buy firewood. There is plenty of wood in the orchard, just take it. She promises that she will ask the *campesinos* to bring olive wood from the orchard and put it near the house. We walk the land gathering wood. We're not sure if there will be enough for next winter but it should be plenty for the spring.

One Monday evening the wind has finally died down. It's a beautiful warm spring evening. We decide to drive to *L'Ampolla* and walk the marina looking at the boats. We look at restaurant menus for future reference and stop for a coffee and pastry at one of the *patisseries*. After eating we walk to the *ferrerteria*, the hardware store, to get some keys made.

As we arrive home the cats run to greet us when we open the gate to the driveway. That's funny; I thought they were locked in the house when we left. As I open the door to the house I can tell immediately that something is wrong. Our clothes are scattered across the floor and our boxes and suitcases are strewn around the room. The window on the back of the house is wide open. One corner of the burglar bars have been torn from the wall and propped open with a piece of wood. We've been robbed! I walk outside to tell Dennis we've been robbed. Heart pounding, I go back inside to see what's missing. The TV and DVD player are still here. I immediately think about our passports. Mine was hidden pretty well but Dennis's was in a dresser drawer upstairs. I run upstairs and see that the drawer is on the bed. It's empty. Oh, no! His passport, credit cards and bankbook! I run downstairs, shocked and angry. We were only gone about an hour. They must have been watching the house! Dennis walks upstairs to see the damage and curiously finds his passport, bankbook, credit cards and two hundred euro in cash under the empty drawer on the bed. Why didn't they take it—especially the cash? Then we notice that our portable computer is gone. It was chained to a metal bed frame with a security cable. They had to rip the back off the computer to get if free. My heart sinks. My writing! When did I last do a backup? I run downstairs again and now I notice that my digital camera is gone. It was an expensive gift from Dennis's parents. They wanted us to share Spain with them via photos. I feel sick to lose it. They've taken the two most valuable things we own. The only valuable things we own. At the back of the house, we see that they used a crow bar to pry the burglar bars out right out of the stucco. The iron gate to the kitchen is damaged but they couldn't get in. I'm heartsick and shaken as I call Frieda and tell her about the damage to the doors and windows.

I drive to *L'Ampolla* and report the robbery to the police. We don't have house insurance for this house but Frieda will need a police report for her insurance. I drive to the *Policía Local* office but no one is there. I go next door to the civic center and tell them I need the police. Gratefully they make a phone call for me, then tell me to wait, the police are coming. After a half hour a policeman drives up and opens the police office. There's no actual address for the house, just a parcel and polygon number. He pulls out maps of the area but the numbers don't match. I search the maps and try to point out the location. He decides that this is out of his jurisdiction and calls the *Guardia Civil*. After another wait, two officers arrive and follow me in their jeep to the house. We show them the damage and explain what is missing. They display little interest until we show them the two hundred euro in cash that was left behind. Then they carry on a lively conversation between themselves shaking their heads in disbelief. They instruct us to go tomorrow to *L'Ametlla de Mar*, twenty kilometers up the coast and file a report at the closest *Guardia Civil* station.

Frieda calls to tell me a friend of theirs will come tomorrow to fix the bars on the windows. She keeps apologizing to me. "I'm so sorry this happened. How terrible for you, first no washing machine now this. I think you are very brave." I don't feel brave now. I feel like the house is being watched, that we are being watched. Every time I leave the house now, I will wonder what we will come home to.

The next day Dennis grabs the Spanish dictionary and drives to *L'Ametlla* to file a police report. I wait for the people who will fix the bars on the window. Just after Dennis leaves two men and a woman pull into the driveway and honk at the gate. I am happy they are so quick to come, without the bars we don't want to leave the house. They inspect the damage and tell me the old bars were not that good, they will put on new, better ones this afternoon. They tell me to be sure to use the pull down shutters and lock them every time we leave the house. I tell them that we didn't think they were important because they are just light plastic. The woman disagrees, "*No, no esta muy fuerte como plástico de avión.*" It's very strong, like airplane plastic. They take photos for the insurance company and then leave.

Later that afternoon one of the men returns to install new burglar bars on the windows and the insurance man arrives. He has driven from *Tortosa* and examines the damage on the windows and kitchen door. He shakes his head and tells me there used to be only one or two robberies a month in this area, but now in the last few years there is ten or twenty a month. Your robbers were very nice he says, some of them are just "*feo*", ugly. They destroy things just to be mean. He demonstrates with his hands, like tearing up the sofa and mattresses with a knife. It used to be the thieves were gypsies who were looking for food or money because they were poor. Now they are people from Eastern Europe and they are organized. They know what they want and look for it. One man I know put a hundred thousand euro of solar panels on his roof and they were stolen. He waited three months then put them on again. They were stolen again. This time he waited one year then put them on and again, stolen. He told me no more. Now he has a beautiful home but no electricity.

Dennis and I feel so depressed. The new bars are on the windows and the house feels secure but it's hard to think of living in a place where you have to be so paranoid all the time. We've been in Spain one and a half years and have been robbed twice. We realize that we are lucky, we didn't lose that much, but it feels rotten anyway. I know this is not a particularly Spanish problem. When I lived in Dallas, my neighbors would get in the car and drive across the parking lot to dump their trash. They were afraid to walk fifty meters to the trash bins. That was in a good part of town. In the ten years we lived in Norway the crime rate shot up dramatically. Every summer when migrant workers poured into Norway to look for work, the Norwegian cabins were broken into, slept in, raided. It must have felt terrible for the Norwegians. But nearly all those cabins were second homes, used only three or four weeks of the year, and the criminals were desperate people living out of their cars. Here in Spain the crime seems to have reached another level. It's not personal, it's a business, it's organized and it seems to be taken rather matter-of-factly by the police.

On the weekend Frieda and Alejandro arrive to look at the damage to the house. She apologizes to me once again. She tells me that she didn't want to put bars on the windows at all, that she doesn't like them but the insurance company insisted. She tells me that even though we were robbed at least we were never in any danger. "Unlike parts of America, here in Spain a human life is still worth more than a wristwatch." I ask why there is so much crime and no one seems to do anything about it. She tells me, "The police arrest people all the time but it does no good. In Barcelona some people have been arrested more than ninety times for robberies but the courts let them go. If the robbery is only for property and no one is hurt then it is not considered so serious. The courts here are very careful not to take away human rights."

Dennis comments, "Well it means that the criminals have all the rights and the victims don't have any."

"I agree with you," she says nodding her head, "and many more people too. They are trying to get the laws changed but in Spain things change very slowly."

Discusión

The weather has been cool and cloudy ever since we moved in but I can tell the summer will be scorching hot. The wild vegetation is sparse, only the toughest survive. There's scraggily wild rosemary, broom and prickly pear. Quack grass lines the roads but is brown even in this cool spring. The native trees are tall, thin juniper and some pine lining the ravines. The rest of the land is cultivated and terraced for olive and almond trees. In *Girona* the land felt lush, every inch covered with vegetation. Here in *Tarragona* the land feels parched. The earth under the trees is baked, bleached, bare. Even the infamous Iberian snail, which has invaded all of Europe, is bleached white, white, white. It's impossible to put a shovel or pick into the ground because every inch of earth has a rock in it. Dennis has been working for days to dig me a garden bed. He's been picking away at the soil inch by inch. Everyday keeps asking, "How big did you want it?" After the first week he shows me a small 4x4 foot bed and asks me, "can you plant intensively?"

Today I was making lunch in the little house when Dennis comes running in the house and slams the door. He was outside digging and heard a loud buzzing noise. He turned to see a swarm of bees heading his way. He tells me he was ready to jump into the pond if they went for him, but they didn't seem to be interested. He came into the house to give them time to be on their way. Bee keeping is big business here. We went to an olive and honey festival in the nearby town of *El Perelló*. They had oodles of different beehives, centrifuges and protective suits and hundreds of jars of honey for sale. There was bee pollen; honey cakes, candy and soaps and if you were keen you could even buy honey in fifty liter casks.

Ice plant thrives here and blooms from April through summer. I marvel at its ability to survive since we've had no rain for the five weeks we've lived here. At night, the frogs sing to each other and our house is surrounded in frog song. Some live down in the ravine, and although I never see them, many live in the ice plant that surrounds the house. I love to stand outside at night and look at the clear stars and listen to the "boop, boop" of the frogs.

I am trying to make a raised bed with rock walls. I'm inspired by the fantastic rock walls I see which make up the terraces of the orchards. There is no mortar in these walls, just rock fitted perfectly together. One or two meters high and hundreds of meters long they must be decades (possibly centuries?) old. Some of the olive trees look like they've been here for hundreds of years. I wonder if the terraces could be as old. After trying to build my own wall I am even more amazed at these terraces. It's incredibly difficult to build a wall that is straight and level. It's incredibly difficult to build a wall that STANDS. The men who built the terraces were not just engineers they were artists. Some of the walls are so level at the top they could have been constructed with a laser level. When Marta and Carlos visit they too admire the walls. Carlos has a theory, "They didn't just sit down one week and decide to build a wall. Probably there was a stone here, then later one there. They were taking care of the trees but always they were watching for perfect stones, for the next part of the wall."

I watch one day as the *campesinos*, the men who work the olive orchard, bring in tractors to pile dirt around the base of the olive trees. They explain to me that when the olives fall they will roll away from the trees; that there's a machine with tines that rolls on the ground and spears them. They tell me life is not as difficult as it used to be, they no longer have to pick all the olives by hand. I'm glad the work has gotten easier for them; nothing is as difficult as farming. It's a tragedy however that the farm equipment is destroying these fantastic terraces. It's unintentional, but when the tractor is driven a little too close to an edge a few rocks are moved, then a good hard rain falls, the dirt is washed away and the rocks fall. Slowly, slowly the whole wall starts to crumble. I can see it everywhere, even in our back yard. No one is repairing the terraces, either. Maybe the art has been lost. I certainly can't do it. Where new walls are needed, concrete is used. Once the damage begins the walls disappear fast. How long will it be before they are all gone? Ten years? Fifteen? I hope I will not be here to see it.

Alejandro promised that the *campesinos* would prepare the soil below the pond for *un huerto*, a vegetable garden. They have keys to the gate so they can come and go as they wish. I started several trays of seedlings, herbs and vegetables looking forward to planting. He promised me they would come the first week of April but they haven't shown up. I've asked them twice when they are coming and each time they have said, "*posible Domingo*," maybe Sunday. I wish Alejandro had never asked them, I don't know whether to dig myself or just wait; my seedlings need to go into the ground soon. I have filled up Dennis's small bed and need more room. Finally, at the end of May I begin to dig another small bed. Now I understand Dennis's frustration with the task, every thimbleful of dirt has a rock in it.

One Tuesday in early June Dennis goes to the tax office in *L'Aldea* to see if they will do our Spanish taxes. Just after he leaves the *campesinos* drive up in a van, open the gate and drive right down to the pond. These men are deep brown and deeply wrinkled from a life outdoors. They are of indiscernible age, old but not old, overweight but strong and tenacious. They drive down below the pond and roll a huge, rusty, ancient tiller out of the van. I walk down to watch but stop in my tracks when I see one of the men unzip his fly and urinate in the garden. The machine they've brought is as big as a horse and these short men have to raise their arms above their shoulders to grab the handles. They are strong though and till the rocky earth back and forth, with the machine kicking out blue smoke and bouncing like a wild bronco. They bring old rusty hoes and with one swish through the soil, they make perfectly straight rows parallel to the pond. They have a box full of seedlings and begin to plant. They make a cut in the soil; insert the tiny plant, then a swish with the hoe to fill in the dirt. By the time they finish the garden is huge, five rows each at least twenty meters long. Then they turn to me and demand water. There's a tiny five-foot section of hose at the base of the pond so I turn this on. They shake their heads no; they need lots of water. There a three inch black hose lying on the ground and they say they need it but it is not connected to anything. There's a drip irrigation system for the oleanders and that is connected to the main water supply. I tell them I don't know how to disconnect it and connect this other hose, that my husband usually does it. There's a timing device on one end and I don't want to ruin it with water pressure. They yell and scream; where's your husband? Why didn't he connect the water? You can't put these plants in with no water! I want to tell them that it would have been nice if we'd known they were coming today, Dennis could have been here; but I don't know how to say this in Spanish. Finally I drag a hose that is connected to the cistern for the house down to the garden and begin to water with that. Together with the hose from the pond the rows begin to fill with water. I have to keep an eye on the cistern and refill it regularly so it doesn't run dry but this seems to appease them and the tiny plants. I can't believe it but they have planted twenty-five eggplants, twenty-five melons, fifteen lettuces, twenty-five bell peppers and fifty tomatoes. Why did they plant so much of the same thing? In Norway, I grew six tomato plants and still gave away fruit. Even if the melon plants only produce one fruit each, what will we do with twenty-five melons? I offer to pay them for the work and the plants but they refuse, in fact, look shocked. I am not sure that this is even my garden, I mean, do we get to eat his stuff or is it part of their business like the olives? Finally, the watering is done. All of us are dripping with sweat. I'm sunburned on the back of my neck but the plants are happy. They load up their mechanical horse. One of them comes to me and plops a bag of fertilizer at my feet. "Keep this here," he tells me then gives me final instructions. "You water, we do everything else."

When Dennis gets home, I tell him about the garden and the problem with the water. He's upset. He doesn't like the cavalier attitude of these men. They come any time they want, day or night and expect us to drop everything and do what they want. He's right, but since neither of us is working, it really doesn't bother me. When he cools off he goes to look at the garden. A little while later he calls me outside. He has connected the large hose to the water system and put in a valve so all I have to do is turn a switch to get water to the garden.

There is little space left unplanted so I begin to plant my seedlings between the other plants. Being a pesto lover, I have lots of basil and plant this next to the tomatoes. I have read these two plants make good companions. The eggplant are spaced far apart and planted on only one side of the row so I put beans across from them. There is a small corner where I plant a square of sweet corn and a shady spot where I put in beets and broccolis and cabbages. I plant different varieties and just a few of each.

A few days later one of the *campesinos, Señor* Joaquim, comes to work on the olives. He always greets me with a huge *Bon dia* and a smile. He has a younger man with him today but doesn't introduce him. Before he goes to the orchard, he stops to inspect the vegetable garden. I walk out to admire it with him. I am thrilled and overwhelmed at the work they did. I walk down and tell him I think the garden is beautiful. *Señor* is very upset. He's pointing at the garden, waiving his arms and yelling. I can't understand a word he's saying. Why is he so upset? I keep saying, *"No entiendo."* I don't understand. I'm doubly disconcerted because *Señor's* young companion is making fun of him behind his back, mimicking him by waving his arms and then laughing.

Finally, he points to the seedlings I have planted and tells me: *"Esta malo."* This is bad. Then I understand what he's saying. You can't put this with tomatoes, tomatoes are planted with tomatoes and eggplant with eggplant, you can't put beans with eggplant it's just not right.

"Por qué no?" Why not? I ask but he starts ranting again. *"Tranquila,"* I tell him. Don't worry. It will be OK. He throws his hands up in the air like I am hopelessly stupid, turns his back on me and walks away. His young companion is still grinning. He tries to tell me something but I don't understand it and shake my head watching *Señor* walk away. I wonder if he will ever speak to me again.

To make some amends I decide to move some of the seedlings I've planted. There's some room at the edges of the rows so I move the basil. The beans will have to stay where they are because there is no room anywhere else. A week later the two *campesinos* return. *Señor* Joaquim acts like nothing has happened. He greets me with a smile and a big *Bon Dia!* I'm relieved that he has forgiven me and remind myself that here in Spain, unlike Norway, people really express their emotions. Screaming and yelling is acceptable, perhaps not to be taken so seriously? I remember that even the word for argument or quarrel in Spanish is *discusión.*

Sold!

We've decided to sell our house in *Maçanet*. Although moving to Tarragona has not brought me instant healing, I do feel much better here. I don't think I can live in the house in *Maçanet* again. Marta thinks we should keep it and rent it out but Dennis doesn't like the idea. She tries to convince him that the price will only go up if we hold onto the house for another year. We would also have a tax advantage. If you own a house more than two years then you don't have to pay income tax on any gain. Dennis just can't be persuaded. The fact that the house is illegal really bothers him. Like a constant weight pressing down on him that he wants, rather NEEDS, to get rid of. The question is: can we sell it if it is illegal? How much of the repairs will we have to do? We decide to talk to the real estate agent who sold us the house, maybe she can advise us. Not only does she know the history of the house, we hope that she will feel guilty enough about selling us an illegal house that she will help us.

We meet the agent at her new office in *Maçanet* and show her the paper from the *ayuntamiento* that lists the problems with our house. She reads the letter quickly and tells us she knows about this but it is not a problem. She can see on our faces that we don't believe it. She tries to explain: "This paper you want. It is meant for new houses, not old ones. This is only for getting the water and electricity connected but for you it does not matter. You already have water and light so it is only a paperwork problem. It doesn't matter."

"We were worried that without this permit the buyers won't be able to get a bank loan."

"No, no. There's no problem with a loan."

You mean we can sell the house and it is legal?"

"Oh, yes, there is no problem."

Dennis and I look at each other. We can't really believe it. We have spent hours, no DAYS, discussing the problems. We've worried for months, it's felt like YEARS. We've asked advice from Marta and Carlos, even from Carlos's mother, and it was for nothing. I'm relieved but suspicious. I want to trust her. We tell her to go ahead and put the house on the market.

She tells us she already has a client who wants a house in our price range. Plus she will come to take photos at the end of the week. She recommends an outrageous price. We've read that house prices have increased 10% on average the last year, but she sets a price at a 30% increase. Once again, we are shocked. I tell her, "It can't be correct. It's too high." But she says, "No, It is correct. We can try it anyway."

Dennis says, "Ok, you are the expert. Do you want us to sign some papers?"

"No, no. That's all. See you Friday."

As soon as we get home, Dennis pulls out all the documentation for the house and starts pouring over it with a dictionary. He's trying to reconcile what she has told us with the paperwork. A few minutes later he tells me. "The best I can figure out is that they have used some kind of grandfather clause to get the house legal. I didn't notice it before but the construction date is set to be years earlier than the house was actually built, and the start and stop dates on the construction are bogus. It says here that it only took two months to build. Nothing can happen in Spain that fast. They jiggled the dates to get the right papers. Maybe the agent is right. Maybe there is no problem."

We've started pouring over real estate catalogues again. A week ago we went to a wine tasting *fiesta* in the mountain town of *Falset* about an hour from the city of *Tarragona*. The *fiesta* featured the lovely wines of the *Priorat* region. The instant we saw the area we decided. This is where we would like to live. It's only thirty minutes from the Mediterranean and on the train line to *Madrid*, *Reus* and *Tarragona*. The countryside is covered with pine trees, fruit trees and vineyards, dotted with charming pueblos. We won't start looking seriously until our house is sold but we want to get an idea of the prices in the area.

Looking at the real estate catalogues is so depressing. Once again, there is so little in our price range. Even if we make a 30% profit on our house, after we pay the real estate agent and taxes we will still be in the low end of the market.

At the end of the week Dennis drives to *Maçanet* to clip weeds, water, meet our real estate agent and have our mail forwarded. The roses have recovered and are blooming profusely. The big root balls I found last year have grown into stunning yellow and orange striped cannas. Dennis will keep the garden watered in hopes it will help the house to sell. It's a three-hour trip each way and he stays overnight one night to make the day less arduous. I don't mind staying by myself but I worry about him making that drive. Although he makes a loop around Barcelona, the traffic is always horrendous and I hate to see him do it by himself. He will have to do this every couple of weeks until we sell the house.

After a few weeks, the weather has turned hot and dry. Dennis goes back to *Maçanet* for his watering trip and to find out what is happening with our mail. He calls to tell me that our real estate agent was showing our house to someone when he arrived.

Two weeks later, the house is sold. The buyers have put 10% down and need to wait for the bank to do the paperwork on their loan. We should close on the house in about six weeks. What about the price? We expected to negotiate a lower price. We never expected anyone to pay the asking price, but the real estate agent says there was no negotiation. The price is fine.

We feel so lucky. We don't feel a single moment of regret about selling that little house. We can start to look at a new house to buy; we hope in the wine country.

Pow! Pow! in the Middle of the Night

We've been walking around our neighborhood and there seems to be nothing but olive orchards, especially in the valleys. At the base of the hills, the orchards taper off and there are wild palms, century plants, rosemary and yucca. There are two roads that wind to the top of the hill near our house. At the top is a housing development which everyone calls "the Swiss colony". Dennis and I often walk up there and we hear the people speaking German and French. The homes are big and beautiful. The yards are green with grass and immaculately trimmed, each with a cool blue swimming pool. Expensive. The place seems displaced, incongruous with the rough dry land around.

It's early summer and the weather is really heating up. By ten o'clock we hibernate in the house. We keep the blinds closed on the sunny side of the house. One day I walk down toward the ravine to pet Murphy and find a cherry tree full of fruit. Birds have pecked many of the cherries but I immediately grab a basket and start picking what's left. I didn't even know it was here. How has this tree survived with no water for months? We haven't seen a drop of rain since we moved in. I've been irrigating the garden with the pond water and it is flourishing.

Frieda and Alejandro want us to meet the neighbors. Introducing us in this formal way seems to be very important to them. The neighbors live a few hundred meters up the road. One weekend when Frieda and Alejandro are visiting, we walk up to meet them. Tall palm trees and juniper surround their house. There's a tiny yard planted with grass under the trees and an overflowing flower garden. This is one of those Mediterranean gardens I envy so much, exotic tropical plants of all shapes and sizes, ceramic pots with splashes of color from incredible flowers. I have no idea what most of them are and can hardly believe they are real. I want to touch them just to make sure they are not plastic. The garden is not pristine by any means. There are stacks of plastic trays and buckets, broken clay pots and burlap sacks interspersed with the plants. The driveway is dirt and the fence is droopy in places but the atmosphere is calm, peaceful, welcoming.

Frieda yells at the gate and *Señora* Trina emerges from the narrow doorway. She's a classic Spanish grandmother figure in a flowered housedress and apron. She gives Frieda a warm kiss on each cheek. Frieda turns to introduce us and explains that we will be neighbors. She invites us into the house but first I point to her garden and tell her I think it is beautiful. She turns and points here and there proudly naming a few plants. Frieda explains that *Señora* is very good with plants but her husband is an expert. Anything I want to know, just ask him. He's worked at a nursery in *Tortosa* for thirty years.

Inside the house is one large kitchen/living/dining room. Old sofas line the walls and a large table dominates the center of the room. There's an open fire at waist height in the corner of the kitchen and a dilapidated wood stove near the doorway that's glowing with coals, the door slightly cracked. The room is warm and smoky. *Señora* offers us drinks but we decline. I ask if they live here all year round but she shakes her head no. She cares for her grandchildren during the week and only comes out on the weekends. Frieda explains that *Señora* is a traditional Spanish grandmother. "This is the way families have been in Spain for centuries. The grandmother takes care of the grandchildren while the parents work." She translates for *Señora* who beams, obviously satisfied with the explanation. *Señor* Juan comes in with Alejandro and we are introduced. He hurries back outside and returns with his arms full of artichokes. There's a quick discussion and suddenly it's decided that we are all staying for lunch.

Señora Trina starts to prepare the artichokes and I move to the kitchen to watch her. I tell her I want to learn. Frieda joins us and tells me that *Señora* is an excellent cook. *Señora* trims the artichoke stems then turns each one upside down and pounds the top quite hard against the table. She spreads the top open, pours in olive oil and large pinches of salt then carefully places them upright in the coals of the fireplace. *Esta*! That's it.

Alejandro and *Señor* Juan have gone back outside. They return with a large black bucket and a dead bird. *Señor* starts to pluck the bird and I turn my face away. "*No puedo*," I say, I can't watch. Frieda agrees with me, "*mi tampoco*," me neither. Alejandro explains that they are both hunters. This is the bird that goes "coo, coo." There are small feathers flying around the room, sticking to the sofa, the chairs and my sweater. Dennis turns to me and he smiles. He doesn't say anything aloud but I can hear the message loud and clear—quite a culture shock isn't it?

Frieda sets the table with plates that are chipped and cracked. They are different sizes and mismatched. The wine glasses are simple, short water glasses. There's no pretension and no formalities here. *Señora* places a salad in the middle of the table. We use our forks to stab pieces of lettuce, tomato, diced onion, canned white asparagus and green olives. She serves wine from a ceramic jug and tells us it's from the *bodega* in the small of town of *El Perelló*. *Señora* serves a chicken (coo coo bird?) soup that has tiny pasta and meatballs. It's delicious. She gives me a huge bowl full and I tell her it's too much. Then she insists that I need to eat more and adds another ladle to my bowl. Frieda laughs at me until she gets another ladle full too. She tells me it's impossible to say no here. *Señora* puts the artichokes, black and charred, in the center of the table too and we each take one. I'm not sure how to eat it. We normally eat just the heart of the artichoke. I watch as Alejandro cuts his into pieces and eats the whole thing, then I imitate him. They are delicious, the best I've ever tasted. The fire has given them a savory flavor that brings out the artichoke's best. Next, we're served a slice of grilled pork and for desert, an orange and a knife. Dennis leaves his knife on the plate and peels his orange with his hands and *Señora* shakes her head—such a strange habits! We're served strong dark coffee with whisky or Irish cream.

The conversation is mostly about hunting. Frieda has been translating because the neighbors speak in a mixture of Catalan and *Castellano*. She loses interest when the hunting stories start and goes to help *Señora* wash the dishes. Alejandro takes over explaining when we don't understand. I gasp when I hear that *Señor* shoots cats and dogs. Alejandro explains that they don't shoot animals that belong to people, only strays. He tells me that they destroy the native wildlife; then he demonstrates, hunching his shoulders. A cat will sit like this on a rabbit hole and wait. It can wait for hours. They feel the movement under the earth. Then as soon as the rabbit comes out it pounces. Then it sits waits for the next one. He shrugs his shoulders; soon there are no more rabbits.

"I understand, but please don't shoot my cats."

"*Tranquila,*" he says, don't worry. We never shoot within two hundred meters of a house. I try to explain that two hundred meters is not far for a cat. I've read that female cats can roam up to one kilometer and males up to ten kilometers. They wave their hands like they don't believe me and repeat; "*tranquila.*" We won't shoot your cats.

Señor Juan tells us that his son just shot a *javelina*, a wild boar. It's delicious he says. I wonder if that's what we've just eaten. Then he describes the hunt. There's an old car in the olive orchard. We put food in there and sit and wait. Then he demonstrates with his hands Pow! Pow!

It seems unfair to me to lure these animals with food. I ask if it works more than once. Don't the animals learn it's not safe? No, he tells me, after two or three weeks they forget. If you hear Pow! Pow! In the middle of the night, don't worry. Don't come running. It's only me or my son hunting.

After, the conversation dwindles. *Señor* Juan falls asleep at the table. Alejandro leans over to explain. He needs to rest. He is seventy-six years old. He has pulmonary emphysema and his body needs the rest. I had no idea he was sick. He seems so healthy. Alejandro tells me *Señor Juan* takes oxygen every evening. Frieda returns from doing the dishes and whispers in my ear, "last year he was very sick with *la gripe*. We thought he would die. He and *Señora* are very close. We are afraid when he goes, she will go soon after."

Alejandro asks what we think of the health care system in the USA. Dennis explains that the quality is good but unless you are rich or very poor, you can't access it. "If we went back now we wouldn't have any basic health care. Maybe we could buy something for an emergency, a catastrophe, but that's all. The insurance is too expensive if you don't get it through your job."

Yes, Alejandro says, I understand. I have worked there. There are some very good doctors there. They are good at research. They have lots of equipment but I think it is strange how they treat people. I worked with infants, newborns. I worked with many different doctors in many different hospitals. They act like the child is not there. They are moving around him like he is just another piece of equipment, not talking to him. Here in Spain I would know the child, the mother, father, grandparents, everything about the family. I would talk to the baby the whole time I touch it.

I tell him about my grandfather. He had a stroke and in order for him to stay in the hospital and get treatment, my grandmother had to sign over her house to the hospital. They let her live in the house until she died but she was so upset. It was all she had to give her children and when she died it was gone.

Alejandro nods; "Yes. Maybe it's better what we have here in Spain. I think there is a difference between medical care and health care. There are some very good things in America like hospitals but here in Spain we have health care, it's more personal and much better. Maybe it's because American is young. Europe is old, we have learned that health care is for everyone. How can I explain? American is like a young man. He doesn't care what he does or what happens to others because he is young and big and strong. Europe is like an old man. We see we need help so we want it to be for everyone. Maybe America will grow up."

Tadpole Hotel and Football

Marta and Carlos are visiting for the weekend. I'm so happy to see them. It's an early July morning and the weather is just beautiful so we sit on the patio of our kitchen and eat a long slow breakfast. Jon comes running to fetch Carlos. Elise is stuck in an olive tree and is afraid to come down. While Carlos is rescuing her, I tell Marta that he seems happier now than the last time I saw him. She agrees. He's given up drinking and is eating less and has lost weight so he feels better. "It was so bad for a while that I was sure he would have a heart attack. Just a little walk from the kitchen to the sofa and he was breathing hard. His knees hurt him all the time too."

Carlos returns holding Elise in his arms. She's crying.

"Don't worry." He tells us, "Nothing is wrong, she is just afraid and has to let it out."

A few minutes later, she is off playing with her brother in our pond. They have been collecting tadpoles on and off all morning. They appropriated the cat's water dish and are building a luxury hotel for the tadpoles complete with rocks and moss.

Marta goes to take a shower and I comment to Carlos that he seems to be getting on very well with the children. He agrees. "It was difficult for me in the beginning. Marta and the children were very close, a little group with just the three of them. When Elise and her brother fight she would come to me and complain but when I get angry at Jon she becomes angry at me. I don't know what to do. Now it is better. I learn better how to handle it but it is never easy."

Later we drive to the beach so the children can take a swim. They are eager to jump in until they discover that there are jellyfish in the water. Then they are afraid. We have only been here a few minutes when Carlos jumps up and says he is going for coffee and a newspaper and will be back in a few minutes. I think it is strange because we have just finished a large breakfast but Marta says it's normal for him. We walk the beach talking as the children collect shells and rocks. An hour and a half later, we are ready to head home but where is Carlos? Marta says he does this often. "You never know when he will return. Sometimes he is gone all day."

"It must be hard because you can't depend on him."

But Marta disagrees. "If he is supposed to be home for the children then he is always there but, if there's nothing special to do, he doesn't care about time. I just accept it as a Spanish thing."

When Carlos returns he explains. There were some old men in the bar and we talked about football[1]. Barcelona is playing Real Madrid and I have to see it. I tell Carlos that we only have satellite TV at the house so we cannot see the game live. He tells us, "I will have to go to the bar then to watch it. If Barcelona wins tonight then they are only one game away from championship. It is very important."

That evening Carlos invites us to go to the bar to watch the game. I am the only one interested. Marta wants to stay home with the kids and Dennis doesn't like soccer. I am becoming a real fan though and watch it every chance I get. I tell Carlos that I really like Real Madrid and Barcelona both so I don't care who wins. He is shocked. "You cannot like both of them. They are enemies."

The tiny bar in *El Perelló* is packed with men; young, old and every age in between. We find two bar stools but there are no empty tables. Then some old men make some room for us offering us a small part of their table. The game is just beginning and already the bar is filled with smoke. The crowd lets out a big cheer as the Barcelona team runs on to the field, then boos and hisses at the team from Real Madrid. I decide right then and there that tonight I will cheer for Barcelona, otherwise I might be tarred and feathered. The atmosphere here is electric. At each goal attempt the crowd is on their feet and screaming. At Barcelona's first goal they go wild. The man behind me pounds his fists on the table so hard that he bounces my wine glass right off the table and it smashes on the floor. Suddenly there is a deafening sound. Someone has exploded a large firecracker right here in the bar. My ears are ringing when the man behind me taps me on the shoulder and offers to buy me a new glass of wine.

Back at the house, we excitedly tell Dennis what happened. *Barça* won 2 to 0. The championship is nearly secured! Then we realize that we have to be quiet. Marta and the children are asleep upstairs. Carlos and I suddenly realize we are starving. I go to the little house and cook hamburgers then the three of us sit in the tiny kitchen and talk football.

---

1.   European football is the same as soccer in America.

Rich Man

There is was an old man standing in our back yard so I go out to see what he wants. He tells me that he is a neighbor and waves his hand toward a house on the hill across the ravine. He could see that we were home so he came to say hello. His name is *Señor* Vicente and he's little and frail with deep brown skin, like he has spent a lifetime in the sun. His eyes are warm and friendly and he is lively when he talks, waving his arms in the air. Difficult to understand, he slurs his words and probably speaks in a mixture of *Castellano* and Catalan. I don't understand much of what he says but he doesn't seem to care. Before he leaves he invites us to visit and points to his house on the hill.

It's a beautiful warm Sunday afternoon. I can hear voices from *Señor* Vicente's house. Since I have tons of green peppers, eggplant, tomatoes and melons from the garden I decide to load up a basket and take them over. The basket is too heavy for me to carry so I ask Dennis if he will carry it for me up to the neighbor's house. He gets upset; "No, I don't want to go."

I tell him "We don't have to stay long, we'll just drop them off", but he still refuses. He knows that we will HAVE to stay and visit. I get upset and we argue. Why is he so antisocial? I simply can't understand that he doesn't need other people like I do and that socializing is stressful for him. We've been together for twenty-four years, I should be used to him by now but occasionally I blow up. I'm lonely and it's worse for me here where I don't have any friends.

I spite myself and grab the basket and head out the door on my own. The basket is heavy and I have to keep switching it from arm to arm and stop to rest periodically. There are flies, incredibly persistent and annoying, that follow me to the neighbor's house. Because of the ravine, I have to go out to the road and make a big loop instead of walking there directly. There are two cars parked in their driveway so I stop there and yell, "*Hola! Hola!*" No one responds. I walk to the front porch and yell again. Finally, someone from inside calls, "*Si?*" pushes the beads from the front door and comes out to greet me. The woman gives me a big smile and then I see *Señor* Vicente behind her. He opens his arms wide and gives me a big smile and I lean over and give him a kiss on both cheeks, the common Spanish greeting. The woman asks, "You two know each other?"

I nod my head yes and tell her I'm the neighbor, waving toward our house. "*Si, si,*" she tells me, "*yo se,*" I know. I lift up my basket and show her, "*Yo tengo estos para ustedes.*" I have these for you.

"*Que bonito!*" How beautiful! The watermelon has split. I apologize but she tells me, no, no, it means that it is ready to eat.

Señor Vicente is so happy that I came for a visit, he is beaming and smiling and telling me he has been watching us and wondering when we would come. The woman tells me she is his daughter, and asks where I am from. She translates to Catalan for the old man and he blows a big whistle through his teeth, so far away!

There's actually two small stone houses here standing next to each other and the woman goes to the other house to fetch the rest of the family. Her sister comes to greet me first, I can see they are sisters immediately and this causes a pang in my heart, I miss my own sister so much. Two older women emerge from the house. I don't catch their relationship. They introduce me to a tiny, stately woman dressed in black that they call "*la reina de la casa*", the queen of the house. She greets me with a kiss on both cheeks then they bring over a chair and carefully help her sit. She seems frail like an antique china doll.

They offer me wine or beer or coffee but I refuse. I tell them that I can't stay; my husband is waiting for lunch. They ask me why he didn't come and I try to explain stumbling over my words that he is not social, not a people person. The two young women nod their heads in understanding. They are both married to men like that. The old man jumps in and tells me that it's good to visit neighbors. They have visitors all the time. Even if they have to yell across the ravine, it's good to talk to each other. They are all so warm and welcoming. I think if they knew me a little while longer they would be wrapping me in their arms. I ask if they live here all year round but they tell me that it's only during August. The rest of the year they come only on weekends. The old man warns me that he has an indiscrete question then asks about our robbery. I guess that we have been gossiped about. I explain that they broke the bars on the window and that we lost a computer and a digital camera. They tell me they too have been robbed and show me the window where the thieves broke in. It's a tiny kitchen with rebar across a wooden frame window. They explain that the thieves were very polite. They removed the wooden window and set it carefully to the side then took only a little food, just food that they liked like olive oil and spaghetti. They didn't touch the wine or the radio. I look around the interior of their house. It's simply furnished like our other neighbors house. The house is tiny, perhaps thirty square meters, only a kitchen and living room. The kitchen has a simple Formica counter. There are no cupboards, only shelves covered with a hanging curtain. It has a comfortable, cozy atmosphere but nonetheless I think most of their time must be spent on the covered porch outside. Back on the porch, they ask where I'm from in America. I tell them New Mexico and try to explain that it is just north of old Mexico. They say that I must know some Spanish. I tell them, "*solo pocos, pocos palabras*," only few, few words. Then I explain that sometimes the words I know have different meanings here. A *tortilla* in New Mexico is like flat bread made of wheat or corn. Here it is a potatoes and egg omelet. A *tostada* in New Mexico is a fried corn tortilla eaten with refried beans, here it is toast served with jam. It's not always easy. They nod in understanding.

Then I explain that I have to go. I really don't want to disturb them any longer. They bring out two bottles of red wine and offer them to me. I shake my head no, it's not necessary but they insist that I take them. I look at the first bottle. It doesn't have a label and they explain that it's just an ordinary table wine. One of the women grabs the second bottle and shows me the label. It's a better wine from *La Mancha*. I thank them very much and wave goodbye. They tell me to come again. The old man follows me around the corner of the house. He sees that I don't have my car and he pulls out his car keys and dangles them in front of me. I'll drive you, he offers, but I refuse. I tell him I like to walk. He points toward the south and says, "*mira*," look. He wants me to see that our house is visible from this spot. I didn't realize it but they have a clear view of our back porch and kitchen. So strange, we can barely see their house at all. I ask the man how long they've had this house and he tells me it's a difficult question. He is eighty-one years old, his mother died when she was seventy-six and his grandmother in her seventies. But the house was in the family long before that, it goes back and back until you can't count. He smiles contentedly and tells me; there are rich men who have palaces, big important houses with fancy furniture; but when he comes here to this place he is in the finest palace in the world, he is a rich man. Once again, I'm confronted with that Spanish contentment with life. I look around, at the orchards and the mountains, then down at the sea. I hear the birds singing and frogs croaking in the distance. I agree with him, "*si, es muy bonito*," yes it's very beautiful. He beams.

Doctor Visit

I've been reading a naturopathic book about allergies. After reading the book, I suspect that chemical intoxication is the root cause of my health problems. I have had classic progressive symptoms described in the book and I suspect the culprit is lead paint. In Norway, I spent months and months scraping paint in our old house. The house, built in the 1920's, was old enough that the paint probably contained lead. I wore a mask and gloves but they were very poor protection. I remember, after a day of working, that I had paint chips in my hair, on my arms and even in my mouth. Stupid! Stupid, STUPID, I castigate myself silently. Did I destroy my health for a little aesthetic value? I decide to visit an allergy specialist in *Tortosa*. I want a chemical analysis done of my blood or hair or skin or whatever. I want to know if this theory is correct. If it is poisoning then maybe there's a detoxification program that I can use to help my body cleanse itself. We drive to the hospital in *Tortosa* to make an appointment. Not being an emergency I have to wait four weeks to see the doctor.

The week of my appointment the hospital calls to postpone for another two weeks. The doctor is on vacation. Didn't they know four weeks ago? I have to use this doctor if I want the visit covered by our private health insurance.

I'm very disappointed with this doctor. I can hardly understand a word he says, he speaks only Catalan. Then he tells me I have to stop using my eczema medicine for two weeks then come back for some allergy tests. I tell him I think I have been exposed to chemicals and that I want to be tested for lead. He tells me first we do the allergy tests.

The next two weeks are really hell. The third day after stopping the medicine, my rash returns. This time it's on my calf and feet, on my head, on my back, arms and my hands. Luckily, it takes a few more days for the itch to start in earnest but by the second week, I am miserable.

Finally, the day of my allergy test arrives. I have to wait a few minutes in the hallway outside the doctor's office. I sit in a folding chair next to a woman who immediately starts up a conversation. She has the allergy pin pricks on her arms and shows them to me. Not much reaction. Then she tells me that she doesn't like this doctor. She only came here for a second opinion; luckily, she has another doctor in *L'Amposta*. Great.

The doctor calls her into the office and I am left thinking about whether to trust this doctor or not.

She emerges from the doctor's office, grabs my arm and leans close. She whispers something rapidly about the doctor and *ultima dia*, then says *adios* and turns to leave. I sit thinking about what she said: last day. Maybe this is the last day for this doctor, he won't be working here anymore? Maybe she meant her last day to see this doctor? I'm not sure.

The doctor calls me in. He takes out a case filled with vials then cleans my arm and places drops in intervals in two straight lines from my inner elbow to my wrist. He ignores that there is a big red rash covering the area. Then he repeats with the other arm. Afterwards he pricks each dot of liquid with a tiny needle. I wait in the hall about fifteen minutes then he calls me back inside. He takes out a paper and measures each swollen area and notes it on a piece of paper. He's so difficult to understand and definitely not a talker. In the end, he explains the results. I ask him to repeat and repeat, trying to understand. I think he tells me that I'm allergic to everything; cats, dogs, grass, some kind of plants that only bloom in the spring, dust, mold, trees and I don't know what else. I try to question. I have been a little allergic to these things my whole life, but haven't had these severe symptoms. Why do I have them now? He gives me a prescription for a new eczema cream and wants me to go to a dermatologist. What about the chemical analysis? I want a blood test. "No." Go see the dermatologist.

Want to Go Home?

Because we feel so isolated, we've decided we'd like to live in a *pueblo*. We don't like being so dependent on our car. Except on Sundays we meet almost no one. I feel lonely and disconnected. Dennis is restless and bored. We would like to have a real telephone, Internet and mail delivery. We would like an actual address. If we had an emergency now there is no way I could explain how to get to our house. There are no road signs, no house numbers. The name of the main road in front of our house is, "the old highway between *El Perello* and *Tortosa*." The road is about thirty kilometers long and meanders through the hills. There are no street numbers. I would have to describe the trees, the ravine, the power lines or hope someone knows our neighbor, *Señor* Juan. We've just read an article about country houses that has put us off buying a *finca*. Spain has implemented new European Union regulations that have made it extremely difficult to get approval to renovate an old farmhouse and turn it into a legal residence. We certainly don't want to buy another illegal house.

We've been looking at houses in the wine country of *Priorat* and *Montsant*. Every pueblo we visit tugs at my heart, they are so appealing. Every house we visit repels me. They are dilapidated or dark; dubiously constructed and way too much money for the value.

We have to go to *El Perello* or *L'Ampolla* to make long distance calls. We only have mobile phones at the house and apart from being expensive, the signal is sporadic or non-existent. I have to walk up on the hill behind our house to make a phone call. The call centers (*locutorios*) are hot in the summer, cold in the winter, noisy and full of cigarette smoke. The walls are paper-thin. I can usually hear someone yelling in Spanish or Romanian or Arabic through the thin walls of the booth. I have to hold a finger in one ear to carry on a conversation. Still it's better quality and cheaper than calling from home.

Almost every Sunday I call my family. I love making the calls but feel so depressed when I get home. Tonight I drove the six kilometers to *El Perello* to call my parents and my sister, then drove home again. As I walk in the door Dennis asks me how everyone is doing. Unexpectedly I burst into tears.

"What's going on?" he asks, worried that something has happened.

"Nothing. Everything, everyone is fine. It's just that I miss them so much. We don't really have any friends here, not that we can really talk to. I mean the neighbors are kind and very thoughtful but it's so bloody difficult to talk to them. I only understand a little of what they say. I don't really see an end to the problem either. We have no friends, no family here. We live in the middle of nowhere and even if we do find a house to buy it's going to be in the middle of nowhere, that's all we can afford. I just don't know if I want to stay here. I don't really want to leave Europe but I miss my family so much. We even have a new niece that we don't even know." At this point, I know I'm ranting and I start crying again. I don't know what to do. I'm sorry to do this to him so I add, "I'm surprised, after all these years that I start to miss them so much. I don't know why it has become so important for me to be close to them."

Dennis tells me, "I've read that the older people get, the more important family becomes, especially for women. I've kind of wondered if this was going to happen." Then he confesses that Spain isn't really working out for him. "I don't think retirement is working out for me either," he tells me. "I need something to do, to learn. I'm interested in robotics or math or chemistry but I don't have any hope of being able to go to school or even get a book from a library here. I'm bored. I thought I was ready to retire but I guess I'm not." I've known this for a while about him. I could tell he has been restless and discontented. I've wondered when he would figure it out.

Dennis tells me we can go back to the states if I want but we should be careful and think it over. It's not certain that we can go. He will need a visa. He's no longer a citizen. We will have to move the cats and we will have to leave almost everything we own here. The electronic stuff and power tools are the wrong voltage. The other stuff, it would probably be cheaper to just replace it than ship it. It's a big move. It'll cost a lot. We might not have the money to come back to Europe if we don't like it there.

I'm not sure what to do. We need to think about it. If we decide to go, this is a good time; i.e. before we buy another house. I love Spain but at this point in my life, maybe family has become more important than places.

Una Mujer Solo

Dennis has gone to America for two weeks to visit his family. The trip has been planned for a long time. His sister-in-law had a baby girl a few months ago. This is his first niece. He wants to meet her.

While I dropped Dennis at the Barcelona airport I got a parking ticket. I was so surprised. I parked in the unloading zone for a little too long and there was a ticket on my windshield when I got back to the car. After all the crazy driving that I've seen here and I get a ticket for parking a few minutes too long. This is something that the locals probably know that we foreigners don't; i.e. you can park illegally anywhere, anytime except at the airport. There's no indication on the ticket about how to pay. After I get home I take it to the bank and ask them. The clerk reads the back of the ticket and says there's no account number but she highlights a phone number with a yellow marker and tells me to call and ask. I hate talking Spanish on the phone, especially the mobile phone. If there's a weak signal at all I simply can't make people understand me. I walk up on the hill behind the house, buckle down and make the call. I talk to two different people, trying to explain that I want to pay *una multa*, a parking ticket. I finally reach a clerk who is supposed to give me a bank account number where I can make the payment. She can't find the ticket number or my license plate number in the computer and refuses to tell me how to pay it. She wants me to call back next week.

A week later I repeat my phone call about the parking ticket. I am told that I can't pay by bank transfer. I have to go to the airport and make the payment in person. Since I am fetching Dennis next week I decide to wait and make the payment then.

Señor Vicente stops by today with his wife, the china doll. Our front gate is open so he drives right through to the back yard then gets out of the car. His wife is in the passenger seat but she doesn't get out. He greets me then apologizes that his wife will stay in the car. I lean over to kiss her on the cheek. We stand at the car window and chat in the shade of an old olive tree. It's a beautiful sunny day, the first week of September. He's come to tell me that their vacation is over. They are going home today. From now on they will only be here on the weekends, maybe some evenings. He says he is sad to leave the countryside where it is so quiet. I get the feeling that he loves gossip when he warns me for the second time that he will ask *una pregunta indiscreto*, an indiscreet question. He wants to know if our landlords, *El Doctor* and Frieda, are married. He has heard that they are living together, that the doctor is separated from his wife. I have no idea so I just shake my head, *no se*, I don't know.

We chat about the neighbors (someone might buy the property across the road), the weather (it's been a drought and a very difficult year for the farmers) the price of gasoline (outrageous). He makes me feel like I belong here and doesn't even mind my bad Spanish. I'm overwhelmed by his friendliness. People are Spain's most valuable asset. They are so warm, so welcoming. I'm reminded of something Frieda told me. She read a research paper investigating why so many foreigners choose to live in Spain. What makes Spain so attractive to other Europeans? What draws them and why do they stay? They surveyed French, German, English, Romanian, Polish, and Russians; people from all over Europe. The reasons most people give for coming here is the climate and until recently the prices. The reason most people give for STAYING here is the people. Frieda explained; "I will give you an example. You have never met my daughter but if she gets married, I will of course invite you because you are our friends. Maybe this doesn't happen in other countries?" I agreed with her completely, I couldn't imagine the same thing happening in Norway.

Señor Vicente asks where my husband is. I tell him Dennis has gone to America to see his niece. I can't recall the word for niece but he helps me when I explain it is the child of my husband's brother. He's shocked when he realizes I am staying here alone and exclaims, *"Una mujer solo! Que valiente!"* A woman alone, how brave! I haven't given this much thought. Dennis and I have traveled often with our jobs, leaving the other person alone. I realize it must be unusual for the Spanish with their extended families. I try to picture *Señora* Trina or *La Reina* staying alone and I can't.

He comments, how difficult it must be to be so far away from the family. I tell him we are thinking of returning to America. I just miss my family too much. He agrees, it's a common problem for foreigners. He tells me that he worked for years with people from Romania. They come here to work on the land. They have good jobs, earn money but they always talk about family, about home. Even if they have a good life in Spain it's just not the same as home.

It's a cool rainy Sunday. We desperately need the rain but the weather has brought back my sinus problems. I sit inside watching a tennis tournament in German on TV when I hear a knock at the door. Since Dennis is away, I haven't even bothered to change out of my pajamas. I throw on a big sweatshirt and pair of sweat pants and answer the door. *Señora* Trina is there with a carton of eggs. They raise chickens in *Tortosa* and since I have been giving them tomatoes, eggplants and peppers, she has been sharing her eggs with me. I love the eggs. The yolks are intense yellow and the flavor excellent. She asks how I am and I explain that I have a sinus infection. *"Dónde está su marido?"* Where's your husband? I tell her he is in America visiting his family. She insists that I come to her house for lunch. I try to refuse, I have a headache and don't want to go out but she won't take no for an answer. Finally I agree to walk up at two o'clock.

I shower, get dressed and go out to the garden to harvest more vegetables. The activity actually makes me feel better. When I arrive at her house I yell *Hola* at the gate. *Señora* comes out to greet me and we empty my basket of vegetables directly into the back of their car. She grabs three eggplants and I follow her into the house. A fire is lit in the kitchen and it's warm inside the house. I remove my sweater and sit at the table. *Señor* is not here now; he's up on the hill filling the community water tank. *Señora* lights the gas burner on the stove, grabs an eggplant with a pair of tongs and holds it over the flames until it is charred black. She wraps it tightly in aluminum foil then starts another one. *Señor* arrives and gives me a kiss on each cheek then pulls up a chair and sits down next to me. I have such a hard time talking to them and understanding what they say. I have to ask them to repeat again and again. They don't seem to mind at all. Sometimes *Señor* laughs at the mistakes I make. He is a natural tease and a flirt too. I offer to help with the cooking but *Señora* refuses. When lunch is ready, she puts a salad with lettuce, sliced tomato, onions and green olives on the table, which we all share. Even though I try to refuse they insist on pouring me a glass of white wine. You can't have lunch without wine! *Señora* serves the eggplant, squeezing open the charred bundles and sprinkling them with salt and olive oil. We eat with forks, scraping the meat off the black skins. Delicious!

She serves a Catalan dish. It's like a soupy pasta stew and has thick golden broth with tiny rice pasta, vegetables and large pieces of meat. I sip a spoonful and it is wonderful, rich and satisfying. She asks me if I like it and I tell her, *"si muchisimo,"* yes, very much. Then she takes a large black blood sausage out of her bowl, cuts it and gives half to me. I realize then she was asking if I liked blood sausage. I have only tried it once and the taste is OK but the texture is disgusting. Now I have a huge piece to eat. I'm not sure what kind of meat is in the soup, it looks like chicken on the bone but when I try to cut off a piece I can't. I watch *Señor* who finishes his soup then picks up the meat to eat it with his hands. Suddenly I can see that he is eating a pig's foot! Blood sausage and pig's foot in one meal! Ugh! I taste a few bites of my pig's foot but then put down the meat. *Señora* ignores the uneaten foot and whisks the bowls away then gives me a plate with a fried egg. She pulls out a baguette and rips off chunks with her hands. We eat the eggs and sop up the yolks with chunks of bread. During the meal I have been telling them we are thinking of returning to the United States because I miss my family. I'm not sure they understand me. They ask how long Dennis and I have been married and if we have children. It is hard for them to understand that we have chosen not to have children. *Señor* tells me children are life; it's how the world goes around. *Señora* clears the dishes and she slices a soft dry cake from a bakery in *El Perelló*. She cuts an enormous slice for me and two tiny pieces for her husband and herself. I protest but she insists. She can't eat much because she has diabetes and her husband needs to loose weight. He refills my wine glass. I am still eating cake long after they both finish.

Señora insists that I take food home with me. Then I won't have to cook for just one person. She gives me an enormous pan full of leftover soup. I try to tell her it is too much but once again, she insists. I am learning that it is impossible to say no here. I thank them profusely for the lunch and conversation and walk home with a warm pan full of soup in my basket. I have enough food for two days.

Dennis is coming home today and I'm so excited. I have to get up at 7:00 in the morning to get to the airport in time for Dennis's flight that arrives at 10:00. I want to give myself a little extra time to pay the parking ticket. At the airport, I go to the information desk to ask where I can pay the ticket. No idea. I try the tourist information office, where they speak a little English but they don't have a clue. It's none of their business. When I press for help she tells me to stop a policeman and ask. I can't find a policeman and walk outside to the parking lot. I see a man writing tickets. He's standing in front of a dilapidated red car that looks like it's been abandoned. As I approach he points his finger at me and asks if the car is mine. I shake my head no then show him the ticket and ask where I can pay it. I don't know; he tells me, call the number on the back. I try to explain that I have already called and I am supposed to pay here at the airport. He shrugs his shoulders, doesn't care. "Try the *Guardia Civil*," then turns his back on me and starts writing a ticket. Frustrated I return to the airport information desk and this time I ask for the *Guardia Civil* office. Go all the way at the end to a white door on the right, he tells me. It's time for Dennis's flight to arrive and so I go in the opposite direction to the arrival gate.

There's something exciting about waiting for someone to come off an airplane. The arrival gate at *El Prat* is set up so all the passengers exit through one gate. They tend to come out in groups and everyone in the crowd stands on their toes waiting for the special person's face. Big smiles and squeals of pleasure break out as people make eye contact. I wait and wait and wait through hoards of people arriving and no Dennis. After an hour and a half I don't know what to do. I check my mobile phone and there's one message. I ring up and hear Dennis's voice, "I'm in Frankfurt, maybe I'll be on the flight arriving at 15:30. Hope you get this. Bye."

Bloody hell! What's he doing in Frankfurt? He was supposed to fly Dallas-Chicago-Madrid-Barcelona. What's he mean MAYBE I'll be on the flight? Which flight? It's 11:30 now. I have to wait here for four more hours. I could take the train into Barcelona but everything will be closing for lunch. I might as well try to take care of this traffic ticket and just wait here.

I walk to the opposite end of the airport and can't find the *Guardia Civil* office. There are no white doors. There's another information desk so I stop and ask. They tell me to go to the end and look for a small white door but I can't find it. I make three loops looking in every nook and cranny but can't see anything marked *Guardia Civil*, no white door. This is ridiculous. How can it be so difficult to pay a parking ticket? I walk outside where it is a little quieter and call the phone number on the back of the ticket for the third time. I tell them I am at the airport and want to pay a ticket. I have to put a finger in one ear and strain through the other because it is so noisy that I can hardly hear. The man on the phone tells me I can't pay the ticket at the airport that I have to go to the local police where I live. Bloody hell! I get a different answer every time I call this number. How do I pay this damn thing? What I'm tempted to do is throw it away. I go buy a sandwich, a newspaper and a coffee and sit down for a long wait.

At 3:30, I go to the gate and join the anxious crowd of onlookers scanning the faces that pour through the doors at the arrival hall. It's much more crowded now and I have to stretch to see over all the heads blocking my view. I wait and wait and wait. No Dennis. At 5:00, I don't know what to do. I keeping looking at my mobile phone but there are no messages. I decide to go to the Iberia desk and see if they will help me. I explain that I've lost my husband; that he was supposed to be on the morning flight but still hasn't arrived. She says she can't help me. She can't give me information about a passenger. I shove his flight information at her pressing her to help me. She takes a look, then gets on her computer but just gives the papers back to me. She shrugs her shoulders and says, "Just go wait for him, maybe he has trouble with his luggage." After an hour and a half? I'm not sure what to do. The next flight from Frankfurt is at 9:00 pm. Should I wait or go home? I walk toward the arrival hall and suddenly I see Dennis walking toward me. We run and leap into each other's arms.

I'm holding onto him tightly. "I was getting frantic. I didn't know where you were. Why were you in Frankfurt?"

"You didn't get my message? I called you from Chicago. I paid fifteen dollars for a phone card to call you and tell you I wouldn't be in until 15:30 today."

"No. I didn't get the message but I'm so glad I found you. I almost left, almost drove home."

"I was delayed in Dallas," he explains, "We sat on the tarmac for two hours and it screwed up all my connections. I almost didn't have time to call you from Frankfurt, my flight was already boarded and they were waiting for me. I have no idea where my luggage is. I've been here for hours standing in line and filling out all kinds of papers. Traveling sucks."

Dusted

It's autumn. We haven't been able to sit outside for a few months. In the heat of the summer there were small biting flies that chased us indoors. At the end of the summer we were chased indoors by normal houseflies. Dozens would swarm as soon as we step outside. Dennis tells me he really dislikes this climate. Girona was much nicer. It's way too hot in the summer and these insects make it ten times worse. He can't even take his daily walk because they are so annoying.

Two days ago the *campesinos* came to spray the orchard. They said they were spraying for the flies that damage the olives. One of them arrived on a tractor pulling a big tank of liquid. He was dressed in full protective gear. I went into my panic mode; pulled the laundry off the line and closed all the shades on the windows to keep whatever they were spraying out of the house. If I've poisoned myself with chemicals, the last thing I need is more exposure. The farmers here are careless with chemicals. Although the driver is wearing protective clothing, his friend walks behind the tractor as it sprays with no protective gear at all. There are huge clouds of pesticide shooting into the air and he simply breathes it all in. He obviously doesn't worry about his own health but I worry for him.

I walk outside after they have gone and see that they have retained their old habits of leaving trash in their wake. Empty containers of insecticide litter our yard and the surrounding orchard. I take a plastic trash bag and go collecting. I have done this a number of times before. When they installed a drip irrigation system they left the plastic tubing and packaging on the ground where they opened it. When they fertilized the trees they left the empty bags behind. I don't think they would ever consider cleaning up after themselves. I met a British woman once who was married to a man from Thailand. Trash nearly destroyed their marriage. He would throw trash on the ground even in their backyard and it drove her crazy. When she questioned him about it he could never figure out why it upset her. "What trash?" he would ask. Once on the ground it didn't exist.

Today we can finally sit outside again and eat breakfast. Dennis is eating cereal at the picnic table while I am inside feeding the cats. As much as I dislike the spraying it seems to have taken care of our fly problem, at least temporarily. Suddenly I hear an airplane flying low over the house. Dennis comes running in the house. He tells me that he felt drops, like rain, on his skin as it passed over. We realize it's a crop duster! We scramble to get the laundry inside. I'm furious! How can they crop dust a house where someone is living with no warning?

We wait for a few hours hoping for the chemicals to dry up before we venture back outside. I have to hose down every thing, the picnic furniture, the sidewalks, the car and the windows. I still fume when I think of my vegetable garden. I've been growing organically and now it's probably all contaminated.

Spain is the most environmentally unconscious place we have lived. Perhaps it's the contrast with Norway but I am shocked at what we find here, trash, air and water pollution, food additives, insecticides and pesticides. Marta was teaching English at a company in *Maçanet* that added preservatives to food. She was shocked that the products are called *mejoras*, improvements and the employee really believed that. The neighbor has emphysema and I have seen him outside squirting his garden with pesticides wearing no mask. When I ask him about it, he just shrugs.

Rice Growing on the Delta

We can shop for basics like fruit, vegetables and bread in the small towns of *L'Ampolla* and *El Perelló* but for other groceries, cat food, films or good restaurants we make the forty-minute drive to *Tortosa*.

One day searching for a restaurant where we can eat lunch, we walk by the station house for the *Guardia Civil*. I am still carrying my traffic ticket in my purse so we stop and ask if we can pay it there. The receptionist shakes her head no; try the *ayuntamiento* across the river. We debate what to do. It's probably a fruitless walk. I make an agreement with Dennis, we'll try this one last time to pay it then I'll just drop it.

There is a police officer at a reception desk in the lobby of the *ayuntamiento*. On an off chance, I pull the ticket out of my purse and ask him where I can pay it. He tells me to go to the post office. Can this be right? There is a bank at the post office but we do not have an account there. We are not sure what we should do. The post office is just around the corner so we walk over and I stand in line wondering if this is another wild goose chase. When I show the ticket to the clerk, he accepts it without hesitation. He fills out some paperwork and takes my money. *Esta*! That's it! Who would have thought that the post office is the place to pay parking tickets?

Just south of *L'Ampolla* is the *Delta de l'Ebre*. It's a flat wetland area, lagoon and bird habitat. It's created by the river *Ebro* emptying into the Mediterranean Sea. It's also a huge rice producing area. We do most of our grocery shopping at *Mercadona* in the city of *Deltebre*. From *L'Ampolla* we drive the back roads through the canal lined rice fields. We've been watching the progression of the rice production. When we first moved here in April the *campesinos* were planting rice in the huge wet squares. Later as the green plants began to poke up through the water we saw them wearing shorts, with tall rubber boots walking with bundles of rice plants in their arms, hand planting the bare spots. One morning, driving to the grocery store, I see what looks like huge reddish brown insects crawling over the roads. How strange, I've never seen them before. What could they be? Then I realize that they are crayfish moving from field to field. A great crayfish migration! Now that the rice is mature, golden brown the farmers have begun to harvest. They use combines fitted with large wheels maneuvering through the soupy fields. Perhaps the crayfish don't like the disturbance? The gulls and wild birds of the delta were swooping down upon the fields and roads preying on the migrating creatures.

Now, in the autumn, migrating birds have started to arrive for the winter. As we drive these narrow back roads we see herons, ibis, gulls, terns and black storks. There's a large population of nearly two thousand pink flamingos that live year round at the delta and so I keep a look out for them but haven't seen any yet.

We slept in late today. The weather was cloudy and rainy and the house gets very cold when the weather is like this. It's down to your bones type cold. I woke up at 8:30 and asked Dennis if he was awake. He used to pop out of bed earlier than I, has always teased me about sleeping in. Today he tells me; "It's comfortable here under the covers and there's no reason to get out of bed anyway. What is there to do today?" Alarm bells go off in my head. It sounds like depression to me, especially for him. I have my writing, gardening and cooking to keep me occupied but he has no hobbies other than walking and reading. I thought I would miss work. I was at the same company for eighteen years and I thought it would leave a big hole in my life to not have it. I thought I would miss the mental stimulation, the technical challenge, being needed. In fact I rarely think about it. What I do miss is people. I know Dennis doesn't really get lonely like I do but I suspect he needs the structure of a job. He needs deadlines, obligations. He is interested in so many things: math, chemistry, robotics, martial arts, meditation and all most anything about nature; but not interested enough to pursue anything in Spanish, let alone Catalan. We are so isolated. There are no schools, no universities, not even a library or movie theater in the area. There's nothing I can suggest to alleviate his boredom and so I make a joke. "You have to get up to pet Murphy, it's your job."

Dennis and I discuss and discuss going to America. Where would we live? What we would do if we go back? We make a list of things we think are important about where we live and rate them on a scale of one to ten comparing Spain with America. They come out almost even, being close to family gets a 10 for America and healthcare gets a 0 but that is cancelled out when Spain gets a 10 for health care and a 0 for family. In the end, the two countries are neck and neck, but for me it simply comes down to family, the other things just aren't that important.

We decide to apply for Dennis's visa and call our families to tell them the news. We are planning to move back to America. Everyone is excited but we warn them, getting a visa is a long process and it's not guaranteed. My mother hopes I will be home for Christmas, but I tell her no, maybe in the spring, maybe longer and there is a chance that we can't come at all.

The new eczema cream that the doctor prescribed is amazing. Except for my hands, it has cleared up my rash. It leaves my skin pale and thin almost translucent though and even a little scratching results in an open wound. The doctor recommended I use the cream for a month but when I stop my rash returns. I continue using it, though sparingly. I've ordered a book from the Internet called the 7-Day DeTox Miracle.[1] The book describes a one-week detoxification program that includes diet; vitamins, hydrotherapy and exercise that are suppose to help your body's natural ability to detoxify itself. If I can't get a doctor to help me, then I will have to help myself. Inspired by the book Dennis and I both try the diet for a week. It's even tougher than the homeopathic diet, eliminating chicken and eggs in addition to all the other foods. I do feel good after the diet is over. My rash is unchanged but my skin is healthier and I have more energy. It's a boring diet though. By the end of the week we are both dying to go out for coffee and a pastry. I will definitely do the diet again. I will do anything to get better.

One Sunday I deliver more vegetables to *Señora* Trina. Her son and grandchildren are there when I arrive so I don't linger. I leave the vegetables and head out the door but she stops me and insists that I try some *allioli*, a garlicky mayonnaise. Her son describes how to make it while she grills me a piece of bread. You pound the garlic in a mortar then add a little salt and one or maybe two eggs then you stir in well with olive oil. He says they eat it on toasted bread, on grilled meat and fish. Then he offers, "My mother will show you how to make it next time you come." *Señora* grills a thick piece of bread in the fireplace and then spreads it with *allioli* and hands it to me. I take a bite and it really is melt in your mouth delicious. With the raw garlic I expected a strong flavor but it's subtle and rich. While I eat my bread *Señora* fills a bowl with *allioli* for me to take home for Dennis and puts a big loaf of bread in my basket. Then she goes to the refrigerator, pulls out a plastic bag with different cuts of meat in it. She shows it to me briefly. Pulling out a blood sausage, she waves her finger at me and warns not to cook this one too long. She explains that she has not made soup today. Some friends are bringing *carne al la plancha*, grilled meat, for lunch so she wants me to take this bag and make my own soup. I try to refuse but she won't accept a no. She follows me out the door then tells me *Espera!* Wait! She picks some fresh celery from her garden and tells me I will need it for the soup.

---

1.   By Peter Bennett, N.D. and Stephen Barrie, N.D.

I show Dennis my basket of food and tell him I guess I am making soup for lunch. I can't believe how generous our neighbors are. I take the basket around to the kitchen and take a closer look at the meat. There are no pig's feet but there are chicken feet! I walk to the living room window and yell in at Dennis, "Do you want your soup with or without chicken feet?" He looks up at me in surprise, smiles and says, "I'll let you decide."

I debate whether to use the chicken feet. Part of me thinks they should be used. If an animal died to feed me nothing should be wasted. The other part of me argues, this must be the dirtiest part of the chicken, where have these feet been? I decide to use the chicken feet, the neighbor's soup is always delicious, are feet the reason? It's strange washing them off. I'm a city girl and this feels so barbaric, so raw. The soup broth does develop a thick rich texture. Perhaps the chicken feet really do add something? I have a hard time when I stir the soup though; the feet seem like bony hands reaching up to grab me. I remove them before we sit down to eat.

Breaking the News

We drive to *Vidreres* to visit Carlos and Marta. We haven't seen each other for a few months and I am very excited to see them. We are bringing Marta a big hand painted pot that we bought in *Breda*. It will look wonderful with a bougainvillea she has on her porch. Thinking of moving we are already starting to give things away.

It's a three-hour drive so we leave about 10:00 in the morning so we can get to Marta's house for lunch. I have a bag of apples and topping for apple crumble that I put together early this morning. I made this for them once before and Carlos said it was one of the best desserts he has tasted so I will surprise him.

Marta and Carlos are not home when we arrive but her kids welcome us into the house. They are studying English at school and I am amazed at their progress. They tell us Marta had to go to *Lloret de Mar* but she will be home soon. They are a little shy but eager to entertain us. Elise brings me her pet gerbil and puts it in my lap so I can pet it. Jon brings me the words to a song he is learning for the Christmas recital at school. It's John Lennon's Christmas song. I tell him that he is very clever to know so much English and he gets embarrassed and runs off to set the table for lunch. I ask Elise for a knife and start peeling and slicing the apples for dessert.

When Marta comes home she greets us both with big hugs and kisses. She apologizes for not being home. "I had to go send an email. The renters in my house have suddenly moved out, they found a place to buy and couldn't wait. There was a woman who wrote me last week. She wanted a contract starting next month. I already said no but now I sent her an email and told her it is possible. I can't afford to have that house empty."

I show her the flowerpot we have brought for her patio and she exclaims: "How beautiful!" Then her face clouds over, "You're leaving aren't you? You're going back to America."

"How did you know?" We didn't even know until a few weeks ago.

"I knew last year. When you got back from America after that wedding I could tell by the way you talked about your family. When are you leaving?"

"We don't know. Dennis is applying for his visa and is waiting to get police records from Norway. We don't even know if it will be approved. At the very least it will be early next year!"

"Oh good, maybe we can come down and visit you one more time before you go. The children had such a good time with that pond."

Marta says there is lasagna in the oven and we can eat as soon as Carlos returns. She helps me peel apples and we chat.

Carlos arrives home with fresh baked bread, baguettes and a round flat Turkish loaf and a bottle of champagne. I'm surprised to see Carlos has put back all the weight he lost and more.

"This one is new for me," he waves the Turkish bread in the air, "but I thought you would like to try." He's brought olives stuffed with slivers of almond, mussels marinated in a spicy tomato sauce and small yellow hot pickled peppers. *Venga*, come and eat!

We tell Carlos the news that we are leaving as we scarf down the appetizers. He's happy we will be in America. "I will have friends there to visit. I have always wanted to go there and buy some cowboy boots."

"Are you kidding?"

"Well, yes and no. I want a pair but just to show my friends. I don't really want to wear them."

"In New Mexico, where we are going there are big, big stores with only boots, every shape and size and color and you are always welcome to visit."

Carlos is drinking heavily again. While we eat he nearly finishes the bottle of champagne by himself. We talk about Carlos's new job. He is working in real estate, something he always wanted to try. He tells me that he has bought a new apartment in *Calella*. His mother buys and sells apartments to make money. She made an agreement to buy one direct from the builder with the intent to resell. The builder gave her a good price but then stipulated that it had to be for her or for her family to live in. She didn't want to live there so she asked Carlos to buy it. Then he can sell it and she can tell the builder that she cannot control what her son does. She gave him some of the money to help. Carlos says he has it on the market now and someone is interested.

"Will you make money?" we asked. "If you own it for less than two years then you have to pay income tax on it."

"Oh, I just add the tax onto the price. If someone buy it now then I have money to pay my tax. If no one buy in two years then I lower the price because there is no more tax. What do you think?"

"Don't you worry about being able to sell it?"

"No, no. My mother worry all the time. A person want to buy it now but is waiting for his bank to say yes. My mother call me and call me, every thirty minutes. I cannot sit there and just wait so I go play golf. My mother call me and says, 'What is happening now?' and I say, 'I don't know. I am playing golf.' It makes her crazy but that is how I do it."

Marta tells us she wants to sell one of her houses. She is just having too much trouble renting it consistently and can't keep up with the payments. We encourage her to do it. She is always struggling with money and it would be a relief for her to get out from under that debt. When Carlos leaves the room, Marta whispers to me that he is not helping her at all. He is living there but does not buy food or pay rent or help with the bills because he is putting all his money into buying and then re-selling real estate. Normally he is very generous but his mother lives for money and now she is involved so he is different.

When Marta leaves the room Carlos tells us that this is his big chance to make it in the real estate business. He can't help Marta with her money problems or he will not have enough money to invest where he needs to.

He looks so miserable. What a mess!

Bargaining and Tiny Birds

When Dennis's visa arrives, we call everyone we know and tell them the good news. I call to say good-bye to the Italians, Marianna and Enrico. I call Frieda and tell her we will be leaving when our contract runs out and we arrange to give back the keys to the house. We will give her our beautiful Norwegian pine table that she has admired. She tells she is sad to see us leave, that we could have been very good friends. I agree with her, we had an instant connection that doesn't happen too often in life.

Gavin calls us from England and tells us they heard that we are leaving Europe and going back to America. How quickly the grapevine works! He offers to loan us money so we don't have to move. We explain that it is not the money that the reason is family.

Last of all, I call Marta. I hate to tell her good bye and hope they will visit before we leave. She's sad to tell me that she and Carlos have broken up. The children don't know it yet because he meets them at the house when they get home from school. I think he was feeling so guilty about money and not helping me that he finally just had to leave. He's been so unhappy lately. I guess it is the best thing.

"Are you OK?" I ask.

"Oh yes, I'm OK with or without him really. I knew it was coming. I was happy before so I can be happy again with just me and the children."

Señora Trina knocks on our door on a Sunday in late December. She is carrying six eggs in her apron, a gift from her chickens. I'm always grateful for the eggs. I invite her for a cup of coffee but she refuses as always. She has to get back to prepare lunch. Will we come eat with them today? I tell her no, we have so much food in the house. Then Dennis shows her a sign he has made for selling the car. Perhaps she knows someone who needs a good car? We are selling ours cheap. We will try to sell it privately first, then we will try the car dealers. We don't want to sell it too fast, living out in the country we can't do without a car. We will need to rent one when we sell ours so we want to wait as long as possible.

She says perhaps she has a friend who would be interested. Can she take the paper to show her son? Dennis agrees. When are you leaving for America?

In about a month, but we have to think of selling things now. "*Venga.*" I add, come to the kitchen, I have many things to give away. We have considered trying to sell the microwave, TV and Dennis's power tools, at 220V, they are useless in America; but it seems so difficult. Our phone rarely works and with no proper address, we cannot explain in Spanish or even in English how to get to our house. I show her pots and pans and baking dishes, also a microwave. She's thrilled and says she will take *todo*s, all of it, anything I don't want. Then she grabs me on the arm and tells me you must come for lunch, we will talk about the car. I agree.

There are no more vegetables left in the garden so I walk empty handed up to the neighbors. There's an olive processing plant a few kilometers from our house and the smell of olive oil is in the air, a pungent sweet odor that we first thought delicious but now find nauseating. Olive season is almost over and there are jars of olives standing in brine on the neighbor's porch. *Señora* welcomes me into her kitchen explaining that the men are in the orchard. There's a fire blazing in the wood stove and in the kitchen fireplace. I join her in the kitchen while Dennis sits at the table. She shows me what she is making for lunch. I am shocked to see a platter heaped with tiny birds, no bigger than ping-pong balls, plucked and headless. She explains, "*Está plato es Catalán, nosotros comemos cada invierno*". This is a Catalan dish we eat every winter. We cook them *a la plancha*, on the grill. My son hunted them. Seeing the look on my face she adds, you don't have to eat them if you don't want to. I will make you *salchichas*, sausages.

Her husband and son return and give me a kiss on the cheek. We sit with *Señor* and ask after his health while her son sets the table. When her son joins us at the table they begin a very fast conversation in Catalan, the only thing I catch is that they are talking about our car. Then her son turns to Dennis. Are there any problems with the car? How old is it? How many kilometers? Is the insurance paid? When is the inspection due? They tell us it's very expensive to buy a used car. There are high taxes to pay. The dealers will not want the car, even if they do, they will not give us any money for it. Then the final question: What is your absolute lowest price?

Dennis looks at me and I tell him. "You decide." He thinks for a moment then names a very low price. I'm a little shocked, but he defends himself. "If they buy it maybe we can wait until the last day and we won't need to rent a car." The son tells his parents, "*Esta un bon precio.*" It's a good price. They say OK they will buy the car. We can do the paperwork next week and they will let us drive the car until the last day.

The platter of tiny charred birds is placed on the table. Her son tells us, you don't have to eat these. I killed them, it is not legal to hunt them, but we have always eaten them, so I do it anyway. He pops one of them into his mouth and crunches it bones and all. *Señora* gives Dennis and I each a pork chop and a *sal-chicha*. The wine is poured and, business concluded, we eat.

The next week *Señora* comes with her son to fetch the kitchen goods. She is very excited and has brought me gifts, a beautiful white silk scarf and a hand painted Spanish fan. For Dennis she has a nice pen. We load his truck and then her son hands me a plastic bag. "These are fish, fresh from this morning. I hope you like them."

The next week the neighbors arrive at our house early one morning. We will drive with them to *El Perelló* to transfer the title of the car and get our money. I tell them I will not join be joining them; there is a lot of packing to do. *Señora* insists. We are going to take you to a restaurant. "*No es necessario.*" It's not necessary, I tell her. You have given us so much already. No, No, she insists, I must come.

Heart in My Throat

Deciding to return to the USA has brought one big relief: we will not buy another house in this country. There was an article in the paper recently about twenty British families in *Alicante* who will have their homes bulldozed because they were built illegally. The Brits say they were the victims of unscrupulous developers who built without permission. Another article in the Norwegian newspaper *Aftenposten* said Norwegians were sending complaints to the European Community about enormous bills (up to 100,000 Euro) that they had received for their vacation homes in *Alicante*. Developers had constructed shopping centers and business properties, installed lights, sidewalks and improved the roads and then billed the local homeowners for a part of the cost. The homeowners had no say in the renovations. They were not even informed until the bill was received. This is not illegal; the developers just took advantage of a loophole in the local laws. I'm so relieved that I can walk by the local real estate catalogues without giving them a thought. I no longer worry about the prices, or the potential problems of buying a home.

These last two years have been difficult but, I will be so sorry to leave Spain. I don't want to say goodbye to Marta and Carlos, to Frieda and *Señora* Trina. The smallest things have become so precious to me now. My heart goes into my throat when I walk narrow cobblestone streets. When I look up at old stone churches, see old men in lively conversations sitting on benches in *la plaza major*. When I see little chunky ladies in flowery house dresses riding their bicycles down the road. When the waiter puts a bottle of wine on our table at lunch without asking what we will drink. When the woman at the bakery greets us with a big *Bon Dia* and remembers that we both want *café con leche*. When I hear the *boop boop* frogs in the evening outside our house and see the tiny fruit and vegetable shop with boxes stacked on boxes of apples, plums, pears and peaches. When I marvel at the huge bundles of spring onions and the barrels of olives in every size and color. When I see the big casks of wine with rows of plastic jugs, the smell of the bakery with *barras*, baguettes standing on their ends against the bakery wall. When I see the brilliant pink of the bougainvilleas at the library in *L'Ampolla* or when the announcer at the soccer game on the Real Madrid TV station   screams   GOAL!   GOAL!   GOAL!   GO.   GO,   GO, GOOOOOOOOOOOOOOOOOOOOOOOOOOOOOAL! Spain has inched its way into my heart. Everything has become so precious to me and I know I will miss it desperately when I leave.

The End

978-0-595-39259-9
0-595-39259-8

www.ingramcontent.com/pod-product-compliance
Lightning Source LLC
Chambersburg PA
CBHW020413290526
45785CB00002B/547